MARCH 2007
DEAR FRANCES
TO YOU FROM YOUR
PAPA, WRITTEN
BY A WONDERFUL
RELATIVE, TO
A WONDERFUL
YOU.
XO
MAY YOU NEVER
STOP CREATING!

Footnotes to the Inexplicable

Footnotes to the Inexplicable

A Memoir in Verse

John Whitehouse Cobb

Slickrock Press, LLC

Copyright © 2007 by John Whitehouse Cobb

All rights reserved. No part of this book may be reproduced or transmitted in any form or by any means, electronic or mechanical, including photocopying, recording, or by any information storage and retrieval system, without written permission from the publisher.

Requests for permission to make copies of any part of the work should be mailed to the following address: Permissions, Slickrock Press, LLC, 2102 Jordan Place, Boulder, Colorado 80304-1913

Printed in the United States of America

Library of Congress Control Number:
2006940059

International Standard Book Number:
978-0-9773755-2-3

Cover Painting: Bayard H. Cobb

Photography: Lee Worley

Book Design: Julee Syverson, Syverson Design

Slickrock Press, LLC
2102 Jordan Place, Boulder, Colorado 80304-1913
www.slickrockpress.com

For my grandchildren
James Dominick Cobb and Ella Townsend Cobb

*Live your questions now, and perhaps without knowing it,
you will live along some distant day into your answers.*

Rainer Maria Rilke

Preface

Until the age of 38 when I wrote several tortured haiku, I had not written a creative word. Previous to that, my writing was extensive, but dominated by legal correspondence and briefs, over which I toiled diligently out of fear that a reckless use of a word would bring dire consequences for a client. This fearful precision proved a good discipline, but less than liberating when the muse would ambush me in a quiet moment. This restraint can in part be attributed to my education, for as Robert Frost once said, "School and college have been conducted with the almost express purpose of keeping him busy with something else till the danger of his ever creating anything is past." Add in law school, and the brainwashing was complete.

In the early 1980's I attended a seminar on "Dharma Art" taught by Chögyam Trungpa, Rinpoche, the Tibetan teacher and Renaissance man. He had the scary habit of randomly calling on people for a spontaneous haiku and when the victim would respond, Rinpoche would "work with them" until they were lured into a "haiku moment" in front of the few hundred petrified, but sympathetic, onlookers. I escaped temporarily that day's spotlight. Yet, I went home that night determined to be "prepared" with an arsenal of haiku for the next day. Aided by one or more glasses of wine, and the comforting restriction of seventeen syllables, I put pen to paper and began to write.

I wrote over the next decade largely to explore my own mind, particularly the forbidden zone of the right brain. I kept these efforts in drawers, travel journals, or on scraps of paper, often lost. Except on the occasions in which I wrote a poem "to" someone, it never occurred to me to share the work or even organize them in any way.

Some years later, when I was appointed President of Naropa University (then The Naropa Institute), I began to use the poetic form to communicate or connect in a less logical or sober manner with students and faculty, who turned out to be not merely a captive but an apparently receptive audience. These efforts were greeted with a kindness, if not enthusiasm, that only encouraged me. I glimpsed at times the wisdom of T.S. Eliot's statement, "Genuine poetry can communicate before it is understood." Some of these poems are published in an earlier work, *Searching for the Moment: Poems on Occasion for Naropa University*.

As the reader will note, three threads of my life have intertwined and collaborated with my writing: first, a journey into Buddhism—more precisely mindfulness/awareness practice and the practice of pilgrimage; second, a lifelong curiosity about birds and our shared natural world; and, more recently and intensely, my experience with cancer. The poems collected herein are from the last ten years, when these streams converged for me most unavoidably and powerfully.

So why publish and why call it a memoir? There are, perhaps, too many, and, no doubt, far better, poems about dharma, birds, or illness and death. However, how for one person, the practice of awareness, close relationship to a truly sacred world, and the meeting of one's mortality can come together and enhance a life, might have a resonance, if not be of some help, for a reader.

There was another motivation. Working on another project, a family history, I realized that between my great (times nine) grandmother, Anne Dudley Bradstreet (1612 – 1672) known as "the first American poetess" and my older sister, Sheila Cobb, I could not discover any ancestor out of hundreds who wrote a word that I would term a memoir, poem or piece of fiction. No doubt they kept journals, poured their hearts out perhaps in letters, but all of that remains hidden from me, if not lost entirely.

Anne Bradstreet wrote poems bravely in a time when the social consequences for the woman writer were severe, not to mention the extraordinary difficulties of surviving and raising eight children in 17th century New England. I can feel her encouragement across the generations, now centuries apart.

And, my sister, Sheila wrote wonderful poems when I had little appreciation for them, but without her efforts breaking the waves for me, I don't know if I would have begun to write, much less attempted this collection. Lastly, I didn't want to add to the collective weight of "voiceless" generations, and, face it, my ego would rather have me be remembered as the great uncle who wrote that "strange book of poems" than be not remembered at all.

    Some of the poems are dedicated. Many poems dedicated to others have been left out. I must thank certain influences in my life without which I would be a lesser person. I have been the beneficiary of the Tibetan diaspora following the Chinese occupation. I have encountered many teachers who have been so generous with their advice, guidance and friendship, not limited at all to what we might call spiritual matters, but simply on how to live a full and genuine life. This began with Chögyam Trungpa, Rinpoche and continued with his son, Sakyong Mipham Rinpoche, Dzigar Kongtrul Rinpoche, The Dzogchen Ponlop Rinpoche, and Ringu Tulku Rinpoche. Also, I explored the edges of the vast and uncompromising world of Zen, as embodied for me by Kobun Chino Roshi and Charlotte Joko Beck. All of these masters taught at Naropa and have been most kind and inspirational to me. As the last poem says: I have been "blessed by more dharma…than any bureaucrat has a right to expect – in ten lifetimes, much less ten years/somehow thank you is not enough…" It goes without saying any spiritual errors and omissions evident in this book are solely my own.

    The faculty, staff and students at Naropa have been an encouragement for me from the moment I joined the Board of Trustees in 1985. Their ambition and success at integrating intellect and intuition, study and experience in the educational environment, no matter what field or discipline, curricular and extra-curricular, not only rubbed off on me but caused me to devote the last twenty years in growing the university founded in that educational mission. Certain faculty in the Jack Kerouac School need to be mentioned: Anne Waldman, Bobbie Louise Hawkins, Reed Bye and Jack Collom have helped so much along the way without my ever "taking a class" or paying tuition. Again, they bear no responsibility for any bad reviews.

I am grateful for those who helped me with this book. Max Regan, of the many talents and manifestations as student, staff, faculty, and friend and mentor, spent many hours reviewing the poems and the structure of the work. Lisa Birman, also faculty, student and staff at Naropa, proofed the entire manuscript and put up with my lengthy arguments over each comma. Sue Kemner-Richardson at Slickrock Press kept me and the others working together and on schedule. Julee Syverson of Syverson Design arranged Bayard's artwork and designed the book.

And of course, to my partner, Bayard, for some 37 years of encouragement and journey together; without her, these poems, literally and figuratively, would not have seen the light of day. Also, to my sisters, Sheila and Victoria, who got me off to a good start, and both of whom as cancer survivors have been invaluable sibling companions in recent years. And thanks to my son, Joshua, because he wrote well and with daring, long before his father, and to his wife, Oakley, who sincerely listens, both perhaps a bit relieved that I have moved, at least temporarily, from political rants to poetry at the dinner table.

Contents

The Times of Our Lives

Clipping My Father's Nails 3
Family Silver 7
    Easton Court Hotel 7
    Scorhill Stone Circle 10
The Times of Our Lives 11
    The Cup 11
    Hide and Seek 15
    Déjà Vu 17
    Passing Thoughts 18
    The Age of Entitlement 21
    Merrily Merrily 23
A Night in Paris with My Grandfather 26
Mobius Strip 30
Just Two Guys *(for MIN)* 32
It has Always Been this Way
    A Contemplation at Tinturn Abbey 34
Retirement Symptoms 36
Seasonal Affective Order 37
    Snowfall 37
    Marchwind 38
    Monsoon Mind 39
    July Evening 40
Sweet Dog Down 41
Tiramisu 42
The Pear Tree 43

American Gothic

American Gothic – Manhattan – Winter 1967 47
The Bardo of Iowa 51
    Visa 51
    On Parole 52
    Migrants 54
    Horizon 56
    Kalona Village and the Mall of America 58
How to Tell If Your Number is Really Up or
  How I Ended Up in Iowa on Morphine 61
Storm Surge 69
Golden-winged Warbler 74
Perigee *(for BHC)* 76
Dharma 78

An Accidental Pilgrim

Mountain Zendo *(for CJB)* 81
L'Atelier Cezanne 82
An Accidental Pilgrim 85
A Lesson from His Eminence on the Path 87
Dharamsala Antiphony 88
The Upstairs Room 90
The Passerby 91
Protecting the Kingdom 93
    The Border 93
    The Checkpoint 94
    Unbroken Lineage 95
    Amrita 96
    Garuda 97
La Transhumance de Vallee d'Ossau 98
The Way to Campostella
  Notre Dame du Bon Port 101
Meeting the Teacher *(for RTR)* 103
Standing Ovation *(for CTR)* 104

Not So, Just So

White Pelican 107
Not So, Just So 108
Cultural Paranoia. 113
India Through a Car Window 114
    Birth. 114
    Livelihood 115
    Karma. 116
The Tourist in Room 106 117
Lake Elementeita Seduction 118
Cote d'Azur Vertigo 122
A Visit to the Chatterwood Home at Middle Chagrin . . 125
La Dordogne 127
Toul Sleng – The Hill of the Poisoned Trees. 128

My Window on the Atlantic

Wales: A Glimpse at a Time 137
    Gwynedd Genetics 137
    Skomer Island Elemental 138
    Skomer Island Evolution 139
    Another Narrow Escape. 141
    Pentrae Ifan Tinnitus 142
    Snowdon Mindscape. 144
My Window on the Atlantic 146
Fall Clouds Over Ipswich Bay 148
Adjectives 151
Shanghai'd Mind 152
a/k/a 153
Winter Waves Off Halibut Point 156

Frontier Stories

Appointment with the Assessor 163
A Walk up French Joe Canyon 166
Aravaipa Canyon Ambush *(for BHC)* 169
Ghosts of Skeleton Canyon 171
Cousin Johnny's Passage *(for JTB)* 176
Bladder Cancer 182
Set Up and Take Down or Thank You is Not Enough . . . 183

Field Notes 189

The Times of Our Lives

the blue heron
flew out of my mind

Jack Collom

Clipping My Father's Nails

The Cygnet has moved
to the near edge of the pond
His dark gray down
innocent foreboding

It is an ordinary afternoon.
I sit touching your bed
the soft hum of the circulator so loud
squirm with every itch of the catheter

It is an ordinary afternoon.
Goldfinches flutter around the thistle
a scourge has entered your bones
and you have risen to meet it

We are suddenly too close
I too have cancer yet fail to see it
the flesh, the blood so hot
the beat of our hearts

as we move apart
to a distance crossed only by longing
It is an ordinary afternoon.
the room is filled with the unspeakable

a talk about the stock market
woven with metaphor
we each contribute a line
a chat on the weather

a distant hurricane, the season's last
nearby Bermuda, site of your honeymoon
becomes haiku to hold
a space illuminated, joined

roles reverse, return
in a relaxed uncertainty
the Cygnet moves behind the island
searches deliberately with an inherited ease

a caretaker enters on the hour
a protein drink is declined
without argument
from her or from me

It is an ordinary afternoon.
the urge to sum up together
panic stifles all words
to a familiar silence

the power of attorney long ago signed
lies in my briefcase unused
a shiver at the loss of a buffer
from this relentless advance of time

a responsibility no longer to be declined
a female House Finch streaked dull brown
drives off the Goldfinches
and their unnatural brilliance

the Cygnet calls from behind the island
It is an ordinary afternoon.
Overcome by the need to escape
"I am going down to the…"

I believe I had had in mind the snack bar
"Anywhere?" you ask
I am stopped in mid-flight.
"Can I get you anything?"

"Whatya got." is no longer a question
return to the bedside, you offer me a hand
 "Shall I cut your nails"
no longer a question

on down, below the skin, I cut your nails
you willingly, strangely careless where they land
there is more dirt under this nail
than I have seen before
shortly, they will cease to grow

grit disappears, flung away
in the poetry of the physical
an imminence over the blanket of blue
stretched out over limbs disappearing

hair and nail tossed transcendent
It is an ordinary afternoon.
you become talkative
we are enthralled

cellulose ridges unpredictable
the new moon of a cuticle rising
your patina glows in my hand
core samples of the weather of a life

chronology no longer important, yet
amid a collage of memories
your choice of subject is not random
a childhood in Idaho, Manhattan and elsewhere

a recollection woven
in a gift of the barometer
strangely arranged on a bureau top
amid the small collection of a life

It is an ordinary afternoon.
our chests rise and fall
you confuse my mother with step-mother
kindly, identities merge and flow

at the confluence of our lives
I hold your hand so lightly
it slips from the grasp
long since complete the task

Absolute white, an adult Swan
appears from behind the island
pearls of water rolling down her neck
the Cygnet awkward in her wake

they say the Enlightened Ones
leave their nails behind
of all believed so essential
only the potency of awareness abides

and there might have been the reminder
that delicious declining afternoon
form is transparent
time, just a thought

my past and the future
shrink, shrivel
I miss everything already
for again our lives dwell
in a single clip

October, 1999
Hightstown, New Jersey

Family Silver

I
Easton Court Hotel

Forty years or more have passed
at the edge of Dartmoor
its wild bogs and bramble
remain uncharted

at the intersection of the hedgerows
the route from Chagford meets the main road
thick oddly sloped walls of 14th century mud
or more recent stucco, roughly troweled

it has been there forever
paned windows deeply set
under the brows of thatch
and patches of bright ivy

ancient petrol pump missing in front
rear overlooks a downtrodden pasture
and what remains of Whiddon Wood
the dream of Drogo Castle

I return to the inn
moments seem rehearsed
fresh clues more remembered
than discovered

my youthful signature scrawled
in a fading guestbook alongside
E. Waugh and others enshrined
by the innkeeper to increase the tariff

is it a photograph of my parents
in the garden laughing
so unreservedly
to be unrecognizable

a dream of my grandmother
dressed in black, wreathed in smoke
living with a man, never to marry
hosting writers, never to write

a vine dangles out of reach
of the yearning hand
evokes a history
as if from amnesia waking

of the inhabitants of another time
unwitnessed, glimpsed vividly
between burnished plank
and sooty beam

a candle reflects in a trembling iris
off the family silver gleams
amid the muted voices of the diners
a surprise spring of nostalgia wells up

innocent of pretension
to distill romance
into a spare fondness
for a past

after dinner in the library
acerbic wit and laughter not always kind
emanates from entries
scrawled in a novel flyleaf

a faded monogram on an inkstand
contents congealed since The Last War
wafts a whiff of cognac
to mix with smoke

that for centuries
has argued with the chimney
endless seasons' past intercourse
exquisite, yet unfulfilled

waning echoes
off gilt and leather spines
yearn for a fresh chapter
whether of fiction or of fact

II
Scorhill Stone Circle

next morning, a rain more like mist
shrouds a walk to Scorhill Stone Circle
a path worn deeply in the moor
along the River Teign, to crest the gentle ridge

we come upon that ruinous jumble
left by ancestors in deerskin cloth
crumbles intact in hopeful devotion
to the course of a sun and a moon

as yet unexplained to science
calls me in illiterate wisdom
to what I still don't know
perhaps simple, but never humble

mind-treasure to be stumbled across
it is said the moor's horses
never venture in
but reckless, I leap under

around some thirty stones
each a cathedral of devotion
in a lustration of anxiety
for that to come

reinvigorated, I am
allowed another chance
not to get it right but
a pouch of flint

a renewed credit in time
I might claim as my own
even transmit as bequest
to my memory's children

June, 1998
Easton Court Hotel
Chagford, Devon, England

The Times of Our Lives
I
The Cup

My sister called them forgetting things
we knew them so well
forgot them, only to stumble
on them discovered anew

it summons the eye from behind stacks
monotonous porcelain, modern blue
calls to be recognized across
a peculiar warp of time

the faded china cup bereft of brethren
its saucer once so bold
victims of endless washings
of breakfasts in between times

For we were in love and in a hurry
to get on with the rest of our lives.

So suggestively it sits
white wooden glass cupboard top shelf
artifact of the early years
of five lives intersected around a table

not long ago, in the age of formica
and cast aluminum molding
technological breakthroughs now humbled
by invention and passing tastes

days of tighter budgets, high expectations
enveloped in an English pragmatism
always white and clean
proper, sometimes chipped

of school buses and lunch boxes
hated ear flaps and the specter of galoshes
unmissed commuter trains
in a gravel courtyard, weeded weekly
stands a war-surplus jeep
and a stately grey Plymouth

café au lait, Twining's English Breakfast
Dundee's marmalade
Bird's Eye frozen lima beans
a Life Saver for the sermon
Ovaltine in place of Evensong
a satisfying decadence

two-gun holsters and head dresses
repeated death by violence
acted from instinct to perfection
by cowboys and indians in a time
where both could be right

migraines and a closed bedroom door
a Christmas missed, unexplained
our practicing anger at the nanny
one day, older sister went
over the handle bars
the first to receive stitches
for leading with the chin

the places declared off limits
always to be remembered
in the bed table drawer
a loaded wartime 45
Uncle Ellis' sword cane
in the closet
himself a question mark

a fireproof safe full of files
hides the aberrant and the eccentric
a history of gain and loss
a delicious corruption
over the horizon of our innocence

Still, we were in love and in a hurry
to get on with the best of our lives.

Like its neighbor, the electric outlet
held captive inside the cupboard
as if some carpenter jealous
of the electrician's ascendance
had constructed this vault

later the painter, his co-conspirator
blended it into the backdrop
to the right of the rim of the cup
condemn the socket to neglect

we were anxious for our obscurity
in the back row, the second string
all the C+'s of our lives
yet so ready to claim a future
rush into the mystery

of hormones, of sex and marriage
children, and husbands and wives
the sinister rainbow of One Wall Street
of the published novel
the $24, 000 Question
by which all obstacles be resolved

where a sister and I stand
dangerously innocent on the top rung
hip matching hip to commune
at the shrine of impermanence

and in the noticing
relieve them, us of a transience
as we rushed onward
transcend all temporal boundaries
savor the fullness of this moment

when even the forgotten
was fresh in its discovery
each instant untarnished
free of mistake
perfect, in its prime.

II
Hide and Seek

We were hiding from someone
in the front hall closet
under the belts of raingear discarded
before the reign of Gore-tex
an unwanted mackintosh, or two
drape from a sagging wire coat hanger

a torn paper cover advertises the cleaners
street address, four-digit phone number
no bait, no lure
an assumption you know
where to find them
when you need them

under the coat hooks in the far back
where discarded gifts hang for years
slowly to slide to the floor
to rest before Goodwill
a plaid scarf, an unmatched vest
a furred hat with awkward earflaps

the wearer persecuted as too Russian for the fifties
never to come back to fashion
over to where a leaning wooden racket
bound by an obsolete press
wing nuts secure against warp
and double faults

awaits the retro tournament
in cubist nonalignment
with its companion pariah
galoshes slumped over in resigned disuse
black clips wildly beckon
until the left one found
to be reunited as a pair

we hid only to explore
in discovery so intense, so sweet
a present so untied from the past
yet, a sense of belonging, free
in a construct of time
amongst objects once thought
sterile and discardable

yet a certain fairness in forgetting
where nothing truly passes
from the present life
enriched by letting go
of even the photographs
so static, captive in their frames

III
Déjà Vu

The other day
I was told
and now
I must tell you
of a man
whose brain registers
present moment
as memory

every moment becomes
became déjà vu
all experience
old hat
and a future
that holds
no held
simply the past

IV
Passing Thoughts

My mother-in-law is eighty-five.
She has no memory
of the moment just past
lost forever, vanished
the moment after it arose
now also gone to then

she asks my wife again and again
whether she was a good mother
there are three responses:
Yes, No and a version of, Sometime
if she, that is my wife
pauses freshly to reflect
the question is lost
between lip and ear

but she, that is my mother-in-law
can't remember
long enough to hold regret
or satisfaction
even the relief
the false certainty provided
by a thought

once, I had a thought
this might be freedom
a breeze blowing forever fresh
every port entered without baggage
the cargo of debts, recriminations
the oughts, the shoulds
all jettisoned outside the breakwater

the stomach at peace
for it has forgotten the chili
the headache throbs cleanly
without guilt for the evening before
all an innocence
of new discovery

but the now is overrun
with ceaseless questions
unending re-orientation
to a biography writ
in disappearing ink

no life review
a future adrift
blown off its moorings
out of the tranquil harbor of reflection

I am suspended
without experience
wherefore my paranoia
for a future
yet unseen

as I sit with her on the bench
at the far end of the lawn
in a precious silence
of her contentment
she exclaims, startled by the flowers

a bed of nameless varieties
every shape and pattern
loop and foil
yet conceived by the eye
a hurricane of color
of thoughtless beauty
that strips the time
the recollections of flowers
from our minds

V
The Age of Entitlement

My life expectancy is 85
it's in all the tables
my doctor disagrees
he has seen this cancer
metastasize in 90 days

the world is full of warnings
of our demise
the pill that soothes
also causes heart attacks
airbags deal out the injury

while hanging the latest proud purchase
a stepladder hurls you
through the plate glass window
the brushcutter replete with safety devices
leaves you bleeding on the path

my mind is full of hope and expectation
an entitlement to a Lengthy Life and
then, if truly necessary, a Peaceful Death
but then, science may
save me still

but if not
don't forget
the Afterlife I Deserve
that I strive to describe
in the most vivid detail
inferred from a persuasive verse
the last preacher
or a rich imagination fueled
by irrational fear of surprise

most of all
Not Forgotten
as ashes in the wind
romantically into the sea
or some such place
not even fit for a fossil
Nampa's poetry
in a box somewhere
tennis trophies, including the ugly beer mugs
in a shopping bag in the front hall closet
a plaque painted over
on the back of a cupboard shelf

with my grandchildren
focused on The Future
of football or soccer
of piano lessons and boyfriends
incipient rebellion to The Past
and a pimple that won't go away

VI
Merrily, Merrily

Life is but a dream, we sang
a marvel, considering
the psychological investment
the interminable rowing in a round

I don't argue with my teacher
when he asserts
all is a projection of mind
of habitual view
accrued over lifetimes

my body is my karmic affliction
now they tell me
if I had tamed my mind
I could have been a star quarterback
the captain of the crew
despite my thought
that I was, whatever
the smallest in my class

What about the birds?
the 2500 species seen
the journeys, the places, the sacred sites
no different from the 6500 remaining to be seen
our imagination run wild
hard to conceive
we dream it up together

after all the atom is 99.9% empty
we could easily design a .1% to cling to
but this wealth of biodiversity
sprung from the sophistication of our neurosis
Redwoods, Glaciers
Ceiba and Savannah
hundreds of species of Hummingbirds
each unique to the eye
easily mistaken for God's Work
or the Wisdom of Man

even Lord Time
decay an invention
Everything. Everyone.
happening at once
the heavens, the gods
the realms of hell
geriatrics, pediatrics
cemetery, nursery
co-exist, overlap in parallel
we wake, tire, go to sleep
not out of need, but addiction
to an order of the mind

my Enemy
always to be in charge?
the cue ball
in this physics experiment
to prove up
the theory of dualism
with hideous will
and deformed body
a sentry at the gate
should I attempt to slip
through to the lucidity
past the bounds
of a collective confusion

my Loved Ones
a mirage?
to shift the heart's beat
the river of blood surges
hugging a hologram, so real
a moment accelerates
inertia so real
attachment and jealousy succumb
wind presses on the skin
the limits of the mind explode
into the infinite stream

September, 2006
Bedford, New York

A Night in Paris with My Grandfather

I emerge from the door of my last bistro
ambushed by an intoxication so lush
the superfluous cognac
though my veins flushes
a nostalgia for the never-known

I could walk forever, carried away
on inappropriate leather shoes
a double-breasted raincoat, unopened
umbrella, silk pocket handkerchief
always the tie a little too tight

in damp reflections in the pavement
murmurs overheard under arch and dome
a crusty palette of memories
late evening dreams
held loosely in the left hand

I could walk forever
my grandfather is my companion from the city
smoky profiles mingle with hoarse laughter
wafted from the recesses of cafes
clears the nostrils through to the ears

illustrate the reverie with grandfather's canvas
stretched, sketched behind my eyes
of city parks and carriages
children in white dresses
overhung with trees that brim

with light, the greenest of green
the discovered barn risen from ruins
brought to life in Westchester
a sagging roof, windows empty
door unhinged

infused with the optimism of a hopeful past
as the foreground recedes
to the ordinary man still overdressed
absorbed at the edge of the road
upright in a dance with an easel

we could walk forever
with utter absence of inhibition
a shiver in the summer warmth
the City floods around us and
all overflows into a grand missing

for a courtliness at Longchamps
flowered hats and pouted lips
tailored tails, handsome
not a hair out of place
enter or leave, longing at the edge

I could walk forever unsteadily
your experience as my own
a cigarette, absinthe at Les Deux Magots
wooden table misshapen over hunched elbows
splash of purple for the night

daubs of yellow
an alchemic incandescence
cramped knees, elbows angled
acute wide lapels, ashy
with an unrequited perfection

you sit at an empty table
not waiting, not alone
a new mink brush in the inside
pocket of a worn tweed
stiff yet venturesome even then

a face too aquiline
for rough strokes
the eyes flash darkly
betray a tension
retrospective and rebellious at once

now humble, now caught
by a restraining arrogance
you channel a breadth of talent
into a classic impressionism
only three decades old

we could talk forever
past Saint Sulpice
across St Germain des Prés
through the shut-shop-loneliness
of Rue Bonaparte

turn the corner
in the last window's mirror
I see myself
amidst the clothes
of spoiled children

reflected off spines
of polished leather
gilt titles mock
the confining judgment of a life
echo back the stock questions for a life

did you not suffer enough
to give rise to an artistic anarchism?
were you bridled by
an aristocratic apprehension of form
implied by the father, inferred by the son?

for you could walk these streets forever
abandoned family
profession betrayed
legacy depleted
heirlooms lost

endure the anonymity
of a decorous non-conformity
your white tie frayed beyond repair
all for an unrecognized brushstroke
here and there

I supplicate you as I walk
in a still life, in a sick bed
on a visit to an eccentric grandfather
thinned hair and faded silk pajamas
the tawdry jokes ramble

before dawn to a child
imprisoned by oils
stacked six rows deep
unframed, some unfinished
all at the feet of the Muse

I could write forever
frightened, longing to belong
to speak to you through a cipher
issuing into the alabaster seduction of the Seine
your Louvre a ghostly apparition

reflected, sterilized in the Klieg lights
of a passing tourist boat
I turn, return spent
to tend to your artist's vow in a Paris hotel
with the streets suddenly empty of you.

July, 1998
Paris, France

Mobius Strip

...on going through Papa's photos at Halibut Point late evening strangely opaque I raise a faded strip of cellophane Old Style Negative, old friend, a young girl, a forgotten corner of a familiar building the present moment before it is gone Somewhere Unrecalled memory starts at a phrase in a poem that reached inside an opportunity, the extrapolation of chance into unwanted success a youth in Paris, playing with a father's palette, all the poems unwritten over an unsmoked cigarette, impeccable, proud, yet outmoded, out of fashion, sister in front of the Campidoglia, waiting for me or for life to carry her away, at least that is what we dream my father's warrior vigor, hidden from his children and perhaps his wife in the next frame, my mother's laugh cutting all moods, so thankful for now, I am armed to the teeth exhorted by a younger sister's loyal blond admiration the lust of freedom the bonds of family, an idle tension Ignorance mistaken for Truth like the enigma provoked by a strange animal as it crosses the drive, once thought seen clearly yet the Guide Book provides multiple answers the vastness of a sea exchanged for an uncertain future, perhaps a crystal mountain or a shrouded canyon. No photos of the life-not-taken, a marimba dancing countess in Rio, fantasies without a script or scene, a malarial infested journey toward stone age tribes, a polymorphous perverse Grotonian stand-in the last, my grandfather's horse caught in mid-jump, top hat and tails a sublime posture of another's life if Enlightenment came with the twist of a head, would I see it, miss it, but I do long for it Cheerful now, amidst the shortening light of might have been, neither lies ahead or is left behind we visualize across the gorge to the other side, a roped span high above the falls, the clouds of mist, now gingerly, pianissimo, finally that word Fulfillment, words unused, much less spring to the tongue from memory's recess some scenes are missed, the disintegration of death, the contorted face of birthing, the pile of skeletons of past lives equal to the peak of Mount Meru the novel unwritten by each generation, until now? Bleak material, bound up by an instinctual muscle. What is the unthinking response? Intended Hands, Black and White, outstretched to raise me, of risks shunned, limited generosity and an attempted comeback fallen short, of what and whom? of lives extinguished before me, of another generation, then mine Whitney, Clark, and now Naiman, et al., et al. All the unspoken rituals, mumbled pleasantries, stale-smoky poolrooms hazy with intoxication of fawned fearlessness, of generational legacy of neurosis a mnemonic key, the Grail of Insight, an unseen magnet orders this genetic happenstance like these nouns and verbs sprinkled onto the page the unthinking, we say, Gannet soars, dives reckless, Eider appear to smile around the mussel's razor's edge, at me do you think? Not yet at the end of the reel, not convinced it is endless, I remain somewhat unruffled, obsessed over the chart with its reefs and shallows, the turquoise soundings of a life on going...

November, 2003
Halibut Point
Rockport, Massachusetts

Just Two Guys
(for MIN)

And we will meet for tea at a corner table
purified by an understanding so stable
a satisfaction so fragile
two guys with a will to embrace

friendship based on no assumption
no school tie, no alliance of family or work
jew and gentile, like everyone else
just two guys dancing near the edge of life

for we have done, all the deals replete
all the negotiations endless and repeated
and we can still wrestle with the best of them
as two guys show off to the crowd

we have seen all the buildings erected
all the insurance claims defeated
thousands of closings so satisfied
but these two guys never look back

hear your voice as it softened
see your smile as it strengthened
your cheeks as they paled
hold light the world between your shoulders

step near the threshold, turn and greet me
you are so thin for the eye of the needle
yearning to throw off my backpack
and join as two guys who shake the habits

as your heart crosses the border
I long to give you mine
have your heart in exchange
two guys just doing a deal

Yes, you are complete as No longer you
for a second, I am no longer I
just a smile and a bow of generosity
two guys who never say goodbye

remember that smile of a last friend
a fond lesson from a fast friend
that we are wise beyond our beliefs
and this time you let me pick up the check

December, 2005
Boulder, Colorado

It has Always Been this Way
A Contemplation at Tinturn Abbey

Eleventh Century Cistercians flee toward a renewed rigor
seeking a pure churchless god in the Valley of the Wye

recoil from centuries of chaos of barbarian bloodletting
darkness rushing into the vacuum of a Roman abdication

a wave of Islam rooting out faithlessness with curve-hardened steel
destroys Nalanda University, teetering in its own imbalance

confident in the restoration of a single solitary faith
with a stamp of Peter's seal, Urban II launches the First Crusade

the ultimate papal punishment for infidels, to retake Jerusalem
and rally under the rejoinder of Your martyrdom

as the Norman destiny plays out over a Saxon tribe cornered
in the shadow of that same bloodstained cross

and we tame England from the remnants
of those hordes without a Settled Truth

chased over Wales by the pragmatic Edward First
and the diaspora of a flagging Indian buddha

led by an illusion-warrior Padmasambava
conquers the heretic Bon in the Land of Snow

guided by some genetic fixation to quench an evolving fervor
leaving obese Henry's tax collectors to substitute thorns with gold

Tinturn, Nalanda and all lie in eternal ruins
as the great Cathedral at Cologne rises stone by stone

to await its turn, in a stranglehold of the vines of fate
under ageless green-black cliffs of mists and trees

wends the River Wye, its ceaseless limpid flow
omniscient and unweeping

June, 1998
Tinturn Abbey
Wales, United Kingdom

Retirement Symptoms

You let another drive
and sit in the backseat

belt secure, unshaven
observing through a side window

you don't even flinch deep down
when in response to

what should I do now
your son suggests you find a job

and rather than deflect, mid-morning
a provocative emotional probe

such as: "Will you go for a walk with me?"
and wield logic like a spear

you hear yourself say, almost aloud
"Life is all a matter of love."

September, 2003
Rockport, Massachusetts

Seasonal Affective Order
I
Snowfall

Thirst of an earth
blessed
the dry crystals
of Lha
drape
an ermine brow
and
tracks follow everything
to its place
even the humble junco
need forage
with a jay
there becomes
an expectant quietude
of retreat
of interruption
and of fortune
meadow grasses vanished
snowbound creekbeds
and
now spruce canyons
muffled in white silver
listen in the mechanical stillness
the earth's rhythms
evoke distant sorrows
ever protected and
awake
to the yet unheard.

II
Marchwind

Tree tips presage
a movement
clouds sweep down
with wind on their shoulders
in parallel lines
struggling crows
frantic chirps tumble
blown with flakes
of unseen snow
eliminating all of the good plans
the minds of moles
untouched
seep a remorse
under the sills
of contented couples
sharpening the knives
polish the furniture
and the floors
and leave
with something
an aging perhaps
as the man walks
the canyon
alone
with the dogs.

III
Monsoon Mind

Morning on the west deck
shrouded, I place my toe
in the board crevice puddle
my soul tenses, heaves
a ship in a mist-storm
saturated skin
porous decking approaching
an indefinable liquid sky
the earth is fissured
     from below
carried as we are
on this planet
dissolving in a cosmos
face the horror
of the cellular generic
a monstrous stream
force of rivulets
falling toward a primeval slough
to the cytoplasm still
where life rises again, again
then drawn up
by an unseen guidehand
climbing to the glacier top
brilliant frozen-water view
out of seared eyes
always searching
to believe beyond
mind's horizon.

IV
July Evening

Soft heat breeze
lazy mind ramble
there is essentially no relaxation
    here today
we have missed
the bluest of the bluest
fledged
heart panging
for all the lost
for the dead
or even dying
road squirrel

there is no solid ignorance
events seep through and in
beyond the gin
a roaring pines' wind chorus
confused
with Flight 907
on approach to profit city

a robin chuckles

in the wren home they are asleep
the plains alight into the dusk over Kansas
the twin-fawn meadow belongs to no one
a slack chin pulls up
startled by the distant horizon glow
and smelling the musk
the proud fox's odor
my mind argues
with awareness.

February – July, 1995
Pine Tree Lane
Boulder, Colorado

Sweet Dog Down

Just returned from the clinic to an emptier place
a Bobwhite called urgently, purely out of the woods
as we put such a sweet dog down

of the same disease I am afflicted, they say
you may have borne it off with you
a naïve hope, yet we shall see

I sit caught up scribbling
then lose a sense of my self
as my right arm drops to fondle your ear

sick body, relentless spirit, you had no argument with time
thrived on the immediacy of perception
even in the glare of impermanence

you hear the leash, a final walk in the tone of it
and emerge from the sanctuary under the deck
suspecting the ripeness of the moment

scratch your stomach once again
say a prayer for your transit, but
your gift is not to question the future

next morning a fattened rabbit feeds near the drive
so casual, the dog's passing
already rung round the woods.

July 5, 2005
Halibut Point
Rockport, Massachusetts

Tiramisu

My grandson stands robust, reckless in the chair
Spanish cuisine spatters his shirt-front
a little prince unpredictable, irritable
lends tension to a comfortable present
a certain lack of resolution

to the sunset over the Bahia Bonita
as it purples out to shadows of a deeper Pacific
the scene is indolent, languorous I suppose
neither anesthetized nor serene
more Cezanne than Matisse

a glass of merlot suspended in delicate fingers
an affordable Malbec, I recall
moustache trimmed, temples more than gray
a glint of ancestral seal ring off the horizon
an appropriate crumple to my white linen trousers

a bougainvillea impedes the view over a darkening strand
where a last egret darts the wave-line with trailing plumes
my family around me smiles on secret cue
as a mariachi band begins to play close by, overly dramatic
I sense a tremor beneath the tableau

our waiter hovers ineptly
aware of a spill on the cloth
nothing left for me, but to order dessert
followed by a glass of port, the thirty-year-old I deserve
in my disquietude, tinged with apology
I calculate an excessive tip

March, 2006
Zihuatenejo, Mexico

The Pear Tree

    My mother
her body wracked with cancer
comes home from the hospital
she knows, we deny
    to die

and propped by two white pillows
with lace around the edges
gazing through the French windows
    day and night
    dawn and dusk
waits for the pear tree
vigorous and straight
in the center of the garden
she had planted some fifty years before
    to bloom

and they did.

June, 2006
Bedford, New York

American Gothic

Let what rises live with what descends.

Edward Hirsch

American Gothic
Manhattan
Winter 1967

He is desperately pale. Skin so thin the eye sockets show darkly through. His ordinarily thin skin seems to have been further flayed by the semester at Columbia Law, not the work, but the stress of it along with his manner of coping. Late nights at Teddy's, sometimes the West End, drink (that year it was 100 proof Wild Turkey), talk and by all means avoid, avoid competing, no not even competing, any displays of ambition. He has looked forward to this party, it had a good address. He was well dressed, and he knew it. Chalk stripe gray suit, custom made, of course, a heavier choice of wool to distinguish it from the off-the-rack version. The four buttons on each sleeve worked, for the same reason, and you could show off a bit by opening the first one. His shirt was almost certainly made to order with a monogram, the choice of collar again distinct.

He spotted her across the living room. It was in the day her last name came most easily to mind. She was the daughter of a well-known, if not famous composer, and, he thought conductor, a Jewish family of intellectual and artistic prominence all supported by some hidden mercantile fortune. To him, she was intimidating and off limits, as well as mysterious and sadly beautiful. He had hardly spoken to her and few of his friends knew her, because of the circles in which she, no he, traveled; or better said in the negative, did not travel. Perhaps, he could get to know her father, although his frighteningly eligible waspishness was an unlikely credential.

He had dreams about her; that is, women like her. Black haired liberals, capable of anything, but somehow restrained by a convention he couldn't recognize as his own captivity. Pale-skinned, but with a luster he could not identify. This was going to end badly, he mused. Worse, it might not begin. While he had always been cum laude at everything since kindergarten, and he had recently for the past month, been cramming his brain full of facts, issues and holdings that had pushed the residue of the humanities over the edge of memory. Worse yet, he did not have the intellect of experience, only the intellect of memory, passionless and dry, even if he had the ability to find humor in the triptychs of the Frick. Most likely, her family had one in their music room.

He should have taken a year off, but the only experience offered to him was Vietnam. The only exit from the hypothetical nature of his life was to kill or be killed. He had not smoked marijuana, but it was his plan to do so in Aspen or San Francisco rather than Khe San. He wondered if his second cousin, miserably picked on at Groton for being fay, as it was called then, whom he heard was flying Hueys into combat, was smoking like a fiend, firing an ungodly number of rounds into a faceless jungle. Now, that was experience. All he wanted to do was tend bar in a relatively safe place. For now he was the envy of all with his draft deferment secure and a leather chair waiting polished in some corner office.

She returned his look without recognition, but the eyes didn't turn away immediately. He began to doubt whether he had met her before. Perhaps he had dreamt of her without ever meeting. Was that possible? He moved closer, and his antennae picked up an unexpected sensuality for which he was singularly unprepared. He relied on a shallow intellect and an aptitude, no an instinct, for delicate cross examination, if not bluff. It had apparently shown through on the LSAT's as well and to his surprise. He could read that week's Time and manage any New York encounter. Yet, he had little schooling in desire, forget long-suppressed animal senses.

He reached her side. He thought with a certain suavity. They exchanged greetings which he didn't hear. She may have noticed his shirt collar. He wanted to ask her if she was with someone, but he persuaded himself it was too forward. Really, he was unbearably shy, and his gambits seemed limited to his clothes and normally his profile might carry the day, but he was also so pale. He detected she was leaning toward him, a microscopic cellular tilt. Emboldened, he was heard to ask, "Where have you been all my life?" How stupid. She did not laugh but smiled, not politely but kindly. "Iowa," she replied, "for research on a paper." His brain went into gridlock. The warmth that had just enveloped his loins dropped 20 degrees. He was doomed. What did he know about Iowa? What did anyone know about Iowa? What was there to research in Iowa, even if you had to live there?

A moment ago he was to convert to Judaism. Now it was over. Failure to express a biting intellectual curiosity in response to such innocent bait was failure. He could not remember anything about Iowa, except the capitol which he hoped was Des Moines. Gaining time, he said with assurance, "In Des Moines?" "No, at the University in Iowa City." She may have been impressed, but she didn't show it, nor did she help him out. Perhaps, she sensed he was floundering, and he had misapprehended the extent of her kindness.

Despite his overwhelming attraction which grew as the relationship became more remote, he didn't care what she had been doing in Iowa. She was really attractive, a certain sullenness in the lips that was getting to him as he thrashed. He began to hope she had a date who would amble over, if confidently, and save him to fight again another time.

This could not be about corn. He was about to risk all with a corn joke, when it hit him. It was about the guy who did the painting. There was a footnote in a text in Fine Arts 13 about it and a slide in one of the few classes he attended. Thankfully, a passing tray of canapés gave him an enlargement of time. But it was gone. Pushed out by the Palsgraf case and the many intricacies of proximate cause, some of which were playing out as he stood chewing dumbly. All he could visualize was Whistler's Mother which was beginning to cause static in his synapses. He couldn't remember where Whistler was from either and that fed his growing ineptness. He barely could answer, "Who is buried in Grant's Tomb?" He countered by repeating, "James McNeil Whistler" to himself, sotto voce almost daring her to put him out of his misery. She did not hear him. She was looking over his shoulder. "My younger sister is here, and I have to take her home. Good to see you." "Likewise," he said as she walked out of his life.

He rarely took the subway, especially dressed as he was. But he was reckless with drink and perceived rejection. It was at 96th Street, it came through. Not Grant's Tomb, but Grant Wood and the sad couple who failed to change his life, mocked him all the way from Iowa.

October, 2006
Denver, Colorado

The Bardo of Iowa

I
Visa

Between chemotherapy treatments, unhooked
Dressed in street clothes, over a hospital shift

Under a frayed Harris Tweed, tubes dangle down his back
Name and DOB conspicuous, irremovable on his wrist

A refugee from the gloom shields his eyes
To contemplate the checkpoint, perhaps unguarded

Down a sterile corridor, he shuffles, dazzled
By a prospect of the western sun of freedom

Behind him, the now empty waiting rooms of karma
From a door ajar, a familiar voice is heard

Brings hastily the olive-green paper unread
That flutters ominously in the airless space

Or is it the hand that shakes in apprehension
As he tenders it to a blurry face behind the grill

For an abrupt verdict unappealable
Based on alleged testimony of an anonymous technician

In a laboratory a thousand miles away
He hears the sound of a computer entry, a stamp falls

A voice says unctuously without inflection
Not kindly, as it is after dark

"Remain in Iowa City a while longer"

II
On Parole

Walk slowly in the middle of the road
Through swirls of last year's leaves

A radiant tunnel of tentative sprung foliage
Telescopes down to the lake edge

A pair of bluebirds arrived together from Mexico
Instinctive partners hunt effectively, a choreography

From limb to ground, and return to sit
Below the dome of green

Approached to a precise distance
They move ahead, immune to our attraction

Yellow-rumps move sleepily in the maples
Most warblers have yet to arrive

An early wren chatters expectantly
Woodpeckers are at work aloft

A Red-bellied call carries over the oaks
Male Downy hammers across the reservoir

The rapid drumbeat liberates skyward
Penetrates the idea of a cloud

Defying the gravity of earthbound lines
Until the IV wound aches, reminds

My foot falls on a leftover leaf
Coming to earth, eyes revolve inward

Not to my plight, but to another
Sensitivity, a welcome wound

The brush of feathers, where
The birds have touched my heart

III
Migrants

Suite 104, River Park Inn, Iowa City
ignored in the AAA guide
stained, forest-green lumpy carpet
we have arrived in the seasonal cusp
between heating and cooling
which means neither works for a week

The neighbor in 102, also a refugee
from something or other
watching morning TV through the wall
they say: when she moves out
they will renovate
when we leave
they will redo 104

They may say this to all the guests
but we believe them
for this is Iowa after all

The end-table indestructible survived
the Great Sorority Debacle of 2002
challenged with all manner of hot items
still ringless
the sofa strives for a faded
elegance in Wal-Mart Tartan
disguises a residue of debauchery

The bisque fridge utters
wounded animal noises
the insurance company calendar
logo removed, the hungry agent
smiles down from
one scene for all the months
brought from Boulder
to mark the days

Windows give out onto the parking lot
where, except Saturday night
few cars interfere with the view
of the lone grand Elm
where the Red-tail Hawk comes
for a late breakfast

Despite his surveillance, rodents
go from here to there on the lawn
he may wait to kill
until we have gone out
for this is Iowa after all

Beyond, are fields
where we walk
long in fallow
full of Clay-colored and a few more
secretive Grasshopper Sparrows

Signs call for its certain development
we mourn its loss
as if we were born here

And returning from the hospital
it is home

IV
Horizon

Heading into the wind, you and I
along the dike at Otter Creek marsh
a blustery sea-level prevailing wind
gusts coldly in the face of elderly pioneers

Gasping for a breath, we walk west
into an unrealized horizon
distant mist, gnarled cottonwoods
guarded by the lighter green
shade of willows below

Destination no longer holds our interest
we become carelessly youthful
appear to waste our time
where a modest sparrow crouches

Golden face, almost amber
thinly streaked sides
I say: Le Conte's, and you agree
as it flies low ten feet
vanishes into the short grass
on the dike ahead

So close
no expectation we will see her again
she has allowed us that one chance
as we walk slowly
no effort to flush her
proudly protective
of her privacy this day

For our eyes tearing
after the Peregrine
gray and sinister, hungry
swoops low
over the cringing marsh
in seconds, beyond our horizon

Coots and Blue-wing Teal emerge
from the reeds, nonchalant
return to their feeding

I am too quick
to identify forms as they arise
but I am so pleased to be full
of lungs and limbs
and eyes and ears this day

We come about
rubbing hands together
adjust our collars
relieved
it is downwind
all the way to the car

V
Kalona Village and the Mall of America

OM
The simple life beckons
a buggy ride into the village
eggs so fresh
still warm from the nest
no transmission lines
bring laziness of mind
wandering of the flesh

An entire village to build your barn
block and tackle, chisel and adze
joinery pure and natural of intent
neighbors always there
but not so close
beyond the last corn row
an invisible comfort

Even the mandatory three-hour chapel in german
a reasonable exchange for a spirituality
of the hearth and harvest
where a banana bread loaf exhales
from the wood-fired oven
no exhaust fumes confuse the nose
preservation is not in the preservatives

The world is confined to a day's ride
amazement lies in snakes and dragonflies
with blue-green crystalline wings
attain the sophistication
beyond the false comfort of addiction
even without a motor in the icebox

Romantic to say
it fulfils
cynical to say
it lacks civilization
for great poets for centuries are
memorized by candlelight

AH
Not far from here
over the Mall of America
flies an oversized American flag
night and day
too lazy to raise and lower
no taps or reveille
where a marine in full dress
patrols the parking lot
like a nightclub pimp

Take comfort America
in the reign of
supersized obesity
manic thinness
indecisive midriff complex
display it, hide it
prudery, degradation confused

Where country folk linger
eat bad cheap food
speak in unintelligible tongues
no longer able to distinguish colors
hooked to cell phone and iPod
while shopping for the necessities of life
sent to us from the Philippines and Bangladesh
and an extra earphone to nowhere
to block out what's next

For $49.99 you too
can be shaved and tanned
as if from Rio
except in the Mall of America
no need to learn the language

Nearby, a Cadillac SUV vies
for a space with a Hummer
late for a movie at Cineplex 64
park closer to french fries and plasma TV
no need to walk to the Drive-up Window of your life

Pigtailed fresh-faced corn-fed honesty
embarrassed for their parents
display their underwear
under deliberately torn shorts
from Indonesian sweatshops
perversely, proudly at the Mall of America

HUM
Overhead, warblers struggle north in May
through downwind pollution
sense the landscape changed
measured since the Fall
they shun the traditional stopovers
press into the fading sunlight
over that which is Iowa
in a still hopeful
imagined america

June, 2005
Iowa City, Iowa

How to Tell If Your Number is Really Up or How I Ended up in Iowa on Morphine

Since everything is but an apparition,
Perfect in being what it is,
Having nothing to do with good or bad,
Acceptance or rejection

You might as well burst out laughing!
         – Longchenpa

The Teacher says
Live life as if you were dying
as in every moment the present ends.

Have I ever been aware of that fourth moment
between all thought of past, future
beyond an inkling of a body in its present form
any confines of a mind even free from thought
a simple present now seems inadequate
to meet the challenge
a rear guard of the past
satisfied and regretful at once
a vanguard for a so-hoped-for future
vivid in its unlimited opportunity

I am at the helm, moments before dawn
Bermuda, whereabouts unknown
the sloop riding each wave with startling ease
momentarily loses the equipoise
shudders down the backside
into a trough
the horizon slips from view
Bow and Stern braced by the sea's turmoil passing
its past and future indistinguishable
the wind is lost and the sails flap directionless

For I would rather be, but I am here
a conundrum is the sinking feeling
anxiety the hoped-for emergence
for an outcome itself the unknown

> *I sit restless in the schoolhouse auditorium*
> *all boys' preparatory school on Saturday night*
> *captive watching 'Bridge on the River Kwai'*
> *near a 12" reel and the only light in the room*
> *The Rector's Hand poised*
> *for pornography to arise*
> *to cover the projector to protect*
> *my mind's screen forever*
> *create a gap of purity*
> *to relish or reject*

He says
Death comes without warning.

When you think you are in the previews
the feature presentation began long ago
illusion is hard to spot
it may no longer be theater
no rabbits out of what hat
no refuge in what script

You used to be able to guess
it was going to end
badly on the battlefield
riding into the sunset
or was it sunrise
you never really had a clue

*I dream again of lying
in the Iowa University Hospital
Procedure Room C on my back
exposed from the waist down
knees held aloft by stirrups
cameras point from all directions
a woman saunters by the back door ajar
waiting for the doctor to run a video camera
up my shriveled member
often accompanied by students
who gather in a semi-circle as if on a field trip
male and female, young and transparent
foreign and domestic, even a gentle Arab
made it to my side through my Homeland Security
and morphine that never seems to take*

too desperate not to undergo the procedure
should staying alive be hellish
I find undue amusement in the ceiling tiles
and have a glimpse of the uselessness of hope

My mind wanders to sentient beings
caught in the web of suffering
I am strangely relieved
as if cause and effect were
the formula of some other god

The Teacher says
Your life until now has been perfect.

Review the humiliations, light
yet so scarring
slights perpetrated to inflate
a pretending confidence
even the triumphs, the applause
most especially the laughter
a rejoinder perfectly timed

*Groton first morning before dawn
forced to take a Cold Shower
by a gay clergyman dorm master
whom I strangely came to admire
if not cling to in front of
thirty laughing twelve-year olds
on reflection they weren't laughing
at me nor with me yet
skip all of the classes, the papers
grades, even sermons
in that moment I wish I had not been born
to recognize the Truth of Suffering*

Enter the clinic receptionist center stage
head peers around the curtain
I am hooked to two tubes
death-defying drip of blue-black fluid
under three blankets
shivering in attempted non-thought

*"Security called. Your wife sent you a message.
She was bringing you a bran muffin
but she is stuck in the elevator – between floors
and apologizes for the delay."*

She tells me the security guards declined
to help her climb out
fear of being sued
the muffin is unscathed
she shows me the bruises on her thighs
having sued with the best of them
I see a discount on my chemo coming

The finance officer of the hospital
is worried about my bill
perhaps, he is worried about me
not being worried enough about my bill
he likes to catch me in the clinic
just before my treatment
waving a promissory note
I hope he will withhold treatment pending payment
but apparently my body is sufficient collateral

He hands me a brochure
setting forth my "Financial Options"
which has a text strangely similar
to the brochure "Living with Bladder Cancer"

> *In the bars in Fort Lupton, Colorado*
> *it is proper etiquette to leave*
> *your money on the bar*
> *during the drinking*
> *the bartender is not anxious*
> *over your ability to pay*
> *and when it is depleted*
> *he may give you a dividend or*
> *you will recognize the moment*
> *get up*
> *go home*
> *and let him keep the change*

One of the perils of being rich
you can have any treatment money can buy
purveyors and charlatans abound
all the results unproven
you could end up healthy and in poverty
rich and dead, even worse
face an endless life in luxury
but prove the Master wrong

I sense Marvin in intensive care in LA
heart, lungs, whatever machine-bound
surrounded by affection, not at peace
my father six weeks dying with a catheter and morphine drip
cancer raging through his good catholic bones
I see the eighteen-year old soldier killed in Mosul
his family bereaved, singled out
graveside in Dubuque

One day at a time, says the Sage

The command is drawn asunder
by the yearning for a limitless future
a grandson playing football in crisp autumn light
slanting across newly powdered lines
all the birds flying unseen
among the slopes of an Andean ruin
a consciousness elusive in a maze of attachments
the clarity of a love without bond
as *carpe diem* struggles with imagination

> *Straining my neck to catch*
> *the orange indescribable throat of the male*
> *Blackburnian Warbler high in the canopy*
> *deliberately he flits*
> *into the leafless frost-bitten tree*
> *just for me*
> *shimmering, doubtless*
> *as if a bird can show off*
> *no regard for its short-lived vulnerability*
> *he catches my eye thoughtlessly*

The Teacher reminds
The skeletons of your past lives
are piled higher than Mount Meru.

I didn't even smoke
DDT sprayed from marvelous
tanker planes over Westchester
running out in my cotton jersey
face open and uplifted to the world?
was it mercury in the spring water at Beauvallon?
asbestos in the plaster ceilings at Waxwing Farm
particles catch the light as they drift to the floor
bourbon and french fries and meat fat
bars full of secondhand smoke

> *Several come to mind, bars that is*
> *The West End, during the revolution*
> *when friends went to war*
> *I believed I was immune*
> *The Catacombs, in Boulder, there's a good one*
> *Harry's in Paris, too overpriced*
> *to stay long enough to be contagious*
> *Casablanca, where the girls were unreachable*
> *and I hid in the smoke-filled corners*
> *the center of the universe, One Plympton Street, Cambridge*
> *where wealth, not health was the immediate need*
> *and I played 8-Ball incessantly with David and Cameron*
> *who smoked and drank feverishly*
> *both now dead, through inexplicable*
> *cellular movements of litigation and Al-Qaeda*

Is it random punishment
retribution for a past long-forgot
taking me to a far, far better place
to fulfill a sublimated dream
even death may be a mental construct
of the mind that seeks to quantify a world
or is life too much to bear

Detach from one's illusory body.
says the Master

One tends to become quite possessive
when tubes are inserted in your penis
to carry chemicals into your kidneys
"Like little fountains, they are," says the doctor
I too should stick to playful imagery, if I were me
laugh all the way there and back
but it makes the catheter tickle

> *Sixth form year reading, I think, Farewell to Arms*
> *contemplate suicide; no, not mine*
> *for I am filled with hope*
> *Hemingway's father killed himself*
> *with his father's civil war pistol*
> *as his son finished this epic*
> *son has just followed suit over my summer*
> *so afraid of dying, he killed himself*
> *to skip the difficult parts*
> *was he ready to die or afraid to live*
> *so much insight argues with so much ignorance*

no comprehending the causes
I strain for comfort
the leash on my vitals
a cramp in my calf
behind a curtain
the man in the next bed retches
senseless selection of karma
happens to us all
one way or another
no matter what I say
statement or question
the Teacher says

Nothing happens.

May, 2005
Iowa University Hospital and Clinics
Iowa City, Iowa

Storm Surge

What this country needs is a colonic
    an Enema from the Gulf
        right up the old Mississippi
Drain the toxins from the river reaches
Wash the canyons of the Snake
Surge up the Rio Grande to its snow-capped headwaters
Rouse the Platte to its former glory
Free the landlocked
    the trout and grayling
        from dwindling algae-choked stream-pools
Float clear blue ice to the foot of the Montana glaciers
Course through the arteries of the continent
Loose the Ohio from its straitjacket
    of rust, rebar and concrete
Wash up the Penobscot and the Kennebec
Storm the dams by surprise
Let the salmon spawn once more
Draw out the residue of the mill town
    feed lot and slaughter house
Flush out the fertilizer of the Salton Sea
Let the Lake Erie invasives drown
    in your overwhelming freshness

The wave of our lifetime
with no one to blame
even FEMA's PR can not explain away
sent not by God nor Satan
no Rapture this
nor Montezuma's final revenge
or the dire consequence of an ignored science

Plunge down the Colorado
    out of the Rockies
    through Glen Canyon
Burst at its seams, down
down deep and unrestrained
    to the Sea of Cortez
once more under the watchful eye of the Condor
your alchemical solution
transmutes the detritus of lead and plastic
with oxygen in the arteries
a sudden intoxication of the system
the country allows its sphincter to relax

Scour the sludge of capitalism
Clean the spectacles of the regulators
Renew history with a transfusion of truth
Rewrite the rhetoric of our self-image
Red White and Blue like watercolors run together
Rock the riverboats of materialism
Baptize anew the churches built on sand

Let flow Sacajawewa's tears
freely over the earth
until Sand Creek, Wounded Knee
and the Little Big Horn
overflow the banks of vengeance
Dilute the hot blood of oppression
with the cool snowmelt of gentleness
in a Ghost Dance of forgiveness

Erase the imprints of slavery as sandcastles in the waves
from Key West to Presque Isle
Rot the ropes of racism
Slip the noose of oppression
the bounds of Mason-Dixon
from the Suwannee to Saint Lawrence
the Rio Grande to the Salmon

Blow out the tangles of hatred
the logjam of guilt
in a flash flood of fearlessness

Power wash the Liberty Bell
Reveal all the warplanes of stealth
Rust the tools of war
Drown the cellars of covert ops
undertow extracts the files of war
Blur the indelible ink of aggression
lush vines ensnarl the conveyor belts of munitions
Soak gunpowder in the casks
Fill the missile silos to depthless prairie pools
where Avocet and Stilt feed in innocence

Liberate the subdivided wetlands
of day-glo ribbons and surveyors' pins
drained marshes, fresh and salt, revived
Redeem the prairie from its sprawl
  for the cry of the Red-tail
  the dance of the Grouse

By your undeniable force
the factories will sparkle
Three Mile Island and Love Canal
all the cities gleam
not from atomic lust
but in unfiltered sunrise
blackwater swamps will rise
sap will flow in the Cypress
the drumming of the Ivory-bill
no longer a mere echo of a vital past
crossed now by an endless migration
  with no memory of acid rain
  or oil-bound shores

insurance actuaries will rejoice
    for their children's children
the Dow Jones will rise in relief
the cycle of abuse severed
trial lawyers stand mute
for there is no provable damage
neither plaintiff nor defendant
can be found

Send the Potomac unrestrained over its banks
Blow the fuses of the Pentagon
down the steps of the Capitol
Float the dollar bills
through the Chambers of the Court
Restore the Bill of Rights to its original brightness
Ruin the Gucci loafers of lawmaker and lobbyist
surprised over their hundred dollar hamburger
so they are compelled to stroll about
in their bare feet with the homeless
made equal in the tidal wave of purity

Gone are the syringes of hopelessness
desiccated trees replenished at the root
in the lightness of a land purged
    of centuries of jetsam
Mississippi haunts replenished
Paddlefish rejoin the ancient, eccentric waltz
Catfish and Vulture can clean up from here

Do not halt your advance
until we are purged
of our constipated arrogance
as patriots, as saviors
the ones chosen by this Blessed Land
as free and all powerful in a Land of Opportunity
Sweep us up
in this hurricane of impartiality
Dunk us all
in the river of clear seeing
leaving us naked
on the shore of truth

then, we may rejoice
celebrate a renewal of our vows
a pristine Thanksgiving
for our Sacred Trust

January, 2006
Fort Madison, Iowa

Golden-winged Warbler

We stand in jewel weed after the news
in a park near the hospital
now a light year behind

desperate for a glimpse of you
a warbler's unabashed love
lifted on gold-barred wings

civilized ears strain for an uplifted chant
to everything in particular
yet beyond reason
you have survived
a million obstacles to return to us
careless
     vulnerable
          exquisite
your brothers lie scattered along the Gulf
your sisters flirt in the fir-tops of Ontario
     miles to go
          miles behind
lurk the winds of pesticide and peregrine
to a destination
you will only know
when you arrive

yet here in a park in Iowa after the news
a surprise resides under every leaf
and you give yourself away in a song

OH, that you would inoculate me
with two ounces of fearlessness
    of no hope
        no memory
innate trust in an infinite cycle

Embrace me, wondrous one
for a fragile moment until the Fall
so I may meet bliss in the meantime

I lift my binoculars
you have gone

May 26, 2006
Iowa City, en route to Denver

Perigee
(for BHC)

May 22 greets us
I drink dandelion tea
from a Wal-Mart cup in Iowa
you play with your Colorado grandson
we celebrate a mutual date
in orbit alone with life

two lovers circle on a beach
intoxicated beyond hangover
a Ground Dove coos with delight
seek a oneness
     irresistible
     ineffable
lured into a plausible scene
the elegant life together
stakes high for the selfish
rewards illusive for the selfless

we engage the boundaries
the irritation of difference
smiles understood mysteriously
equally the grimaces
over ten thousand dinners
each course brand new

I walk the path
a Rose-breasted Grosbeak chants
hidden in a veil of foliage
sense the gravitation of your shoulder
     juxtaposed
     attentive
your cells run in my veins
the chiggers that abound in the high grass
have yielded to fireflies at dusk

Oh, that this illusion will not cease
chased by thunder, cleansed by rain
guests depart and arrive
    auspicious
    strangely tangential
we are vigorous and decrepit at once
for our cathedral has no pews
    doubtless
    joyful
in the faith of no belief

waves roll up the granite shore
to the edge of the moon-driven tide
where the caned chairs remain
bleached in the same sun
casting shadows of our sadness
as each generation folds over us
portraits stare down off storage locker walls
without warning we are elders

grateful for your life's portion given
    undiluted
    evanescent
your profile etched on my heart center
in marriage unaccountable to logic or to time
a Bell's Vireo alights before me
fragile in the spring
to wake me from nostalgia
fill in another piece
of our puzzle near the center
in sound and light we coalesce
    one-pointedly
    joined
alive and in love in Iowa.

May 2, 2005
Iowa City, Iowa

Dharma

The doctor comes through the door
he is always between patients
unstable on a metal stool
a rattle of wheels on linoleum
we are bathed in anxious fluorescence
and tells me I can no longer rely on my future

Lamas have told me this for years
from brocade thrones in ancient rooms
flaking paint of blue and orange
from a worn face beams down
the golden smile of equipoise
yet it all seemed delightfully hypothetical

My mind, ever the merchant of distraction
tries vainly to change the subject
Couldn't you have bought one cheap poster of Hawaii
　or, even better, Venice?

May 26, 2006
Iowa City, Iowa

An Accidental Pilgrim

The first step...shall be to lose the way.

Galway Kinnell

Mountain Zendo
(for CJB)

Crisp call of the Solitaire
so clear, divorced
    from meaning
breath beyond control
melts the wall
    into morning Robin

scuttling robes surround
    no me
trying to extract a last
    reference point
from under varnished wood

somehow unthinking
legs gather beneath me
I turn out
into the still center
    of a whirling age

mimic a bow
here and there so
grateful as
    such dot

suddenly descends
to the tip
of what was
    my tongue

to shatter
my coordinates
in all time
and all space

March, 1998
Crestone, Colorado

L'Atelier Cezanne

Tentative, I step down coming to rest
childlike, two-footing each stair, lovingly
infected by a nearing contagion of his work
being on the stairs he trod daily
    unrestored
    dusty
I could strip off my shoes in reckless
    surprise
    anticipation
as you, in frustration
over an arrangement of the bathers
could stroke a thousand more creations
owing no one, not even yourself

Picture molding vanishes above
in unrestrained gothic shades
an aura of your awareness paints
a present and at once a retrospective
in the haunted dusky corners
the easel-caught spaces
echoes of conversations from within
a bowler hat, a luster of
an elusive fourth dimension
amid casual props
strewn by a curator
a student of these moments
recorded in the air
    imagine
    witness
human gestures even technique
a model's shyness revealed
in the shutters' striated light
the dappled trees overarched play

an electricity of lust in a brush delicate
    extended
    poised
as I long to reach out a wrist, expose
a vein willing to be transfused
to risk all propriety for a sublime
albeit transitory, fix

A creaking pause
a momentary imbalance
as a child newly enabled
    stretches
    peers
upward to an elder's highest bureau drawer
and like thought-absent parents, tourists evaporate
recede tide-like from around me in
    liberation
    revelation
there appears a "Ne Touchez Pas"
yet with courage of ambition
a theft like movement I open a shallow drawer
expecting desiccated tubes
to greet a hazy picture of you
amongst friends on any day posed
Pissaro, your mentor, poseur Bonnard
Monet, last row, outlived
young and brash
peers who know well
it is the Eden of their artistry
    sentimental
    ruthless
anarchic discipline exudes
from confidence in a sensual present
the moment closes
vault like on my exhale

Strange giddiness on the exit stair
I sidle through your front door
stage right a man sketches the courtyard
as if removing a rubbing from a monument
    delves
      desperate
for the formula, a secret alchemy
hidden in transplanted dahlias, a plaster pot
graveled path and stuccoed wall
behind, a wooden gate unhinged
an assortment of tourists
strangely garbed, arranged
on a rough-hewn bench

Glance backward, I visualize
the scene in bold flat strokes
strong bands of odd color
a derangement of shutter
diagonal shaft of sunbeam
warmth radiates
an asymmetric tension in
interlocked blocks of tourists
rise off the bench
all lies in an impossible dimension

Caught in the act, the man
is halted mid-sketch
profiled purple-skinned
    foregrounded
      dumbfounded
an ecstatic voyeur at a
moment of creation
in another's time

July, 1998
Aix en Provence, France

An Accidental Pilgrim

I died several deaths to be here. Drawn not by belief
the irresistible gravity of a place so often sought

where slate cliffs hold secret stories beneath gray mists
shades of green tumble down through vines and cedars

here, a suspicion of holiness lost and regained
permeates the uncut forest slope and the slime and the moss

a rustic cabin smoke-bound holds fast to the shore
no rest for a traveler with the unquenchable thirst

stillness, first leaden now shimmers silver
uncounted prayer flags disappear above in the trees

white then blue faded over green, float hushed prayers
of pilgrims past, over roots and ridge and sky

the mantras, the click of malas, centuries of repetition
held lightly beneath leaf and wing and cloud

mingles with pleas of the hawk-cuckoo persistent
maddening, elusive, high in the trees along the bank

walk slower than ever along the pilgrim path
past a lhasang burner stuffed stone cold with litter

dented prayer wheels aligned along the rickety dock
reaches out over the muck, reluctant to shed the shoes

a man stands juxtaposed with the cabin staring
How long has he been standing there?

touch dreadful poverty, limitless riches
the collected unedited hopes of anonymous seekers

What does he think is going on here!
the lake beckons, there is no need to explain myself

abandon my boots, clouds descend out onto the dock
planks are polished bare and smooth and dark

lest my ignorance withstand the blessings
I crack my skull on the first joist, reel forward

nauseous, joyful to be here, senses relax
confused as to clockwise, a last flicker of embarrassment

stagger down the middle past idle prayer wheels
leave them to spin for the way back

eyes rest above the waterline lightly, luminous
there, two golden ducks glow suspended in a halo

drawn by an enchantment of the senses
caught in a crescendo of insanity and awe

a mind ambushed seeks any cover, yet
the bird book's rationale remains out of reach

the dock, the planking, my grasp
of the rail redundant, I could dive in

the water once shallow and murky
now bottomless, crystalline and leafless

in a relative world stretched beyond breaking
just when I thought I was on a bird walk at Lake Ketcheopalri

March, 2004
Gangtok, Sikkim

A Lesson from His Eminence on the Path

Going down, we meet a khenpo
working his way along the cliffside
his attendant always an equal distance
there is no hurry, no tiredness

his collapsible carbon staff at rest
balanced between thumb and middle finger
it could be a royal scepter
or a yogi's hewn cane

warblers flit through the rhododendron behind
curiosity and detachment in perfect balance on the trail
at the respect of the American pilgrim
rapt in awareness and anxiety

he suggests that a light year can be leapt at once
reminds us of someone we know well
a familiarity we struggle to remember
with a knowing you will never meet again

he touches his worn mala to each head
youth, experience, form and place melt
a vivid awareness with romance compatible
tears seem completely reasonable

a cheerfulness holds them in delicate stasis
how many times has he walked this path?
how many times have I walked this path?
I look back, upwards into the switchback

he moves forward evenly, an old man, without effort
his monk companion almost waves and smiles down at me
there is no film left in my camera
no matter, he is gone

April 22, 2004
Cheri Goempa
Thimphu, Bhutan

Dharamsala Antiphony

Many hundred monks chant a puja
once thought incomprehensible
now knows all language
and I am drenched in the noble truth

> *The choir sings Onward Christian Soldiers*
> *marching in its finery of white and purple*
> *the silver Cross leads them*
> *up the center aisle under vaulted stone*

At the corner of the shrine balcony
vaulting into the Himalayas
the beggars sit in line below
the brilliance and the devastation
blurred in a surge of tears

> *I sit in gray-flannels, always the third pew*
> *for a brass plaque identifies it so*
> *I edge closer to my grandfather*
> *even though I know the liturgy by heart*

Behind me, His Holiness ageless
has leapt lightly upon his throne
there is a roar and a rustle
as the vast chamber reorganizes around him

> *The eagle of Saint John given by my family*
> *wings of gilt and jeweled glare of eye*
> *reassure me, after some struggle unknown*
> *Truth and Love will prevail*

Egyptian Vulture white with black-edged wings
glides below the cornice so close
its bare face glows gold in the sun
my familiarity makes no sense
nor does it give comfort

> *I had silent doubts of Heaven*
> *although often I prayed for my grandfather*
> *to go there when he died*
> *my parents never claimed not to have sinned*
> *but it did not seem cause for worry*

We circumambulate a Sea of Red
waves of monks chanting shoulder to shoulder
through a cacophony of Tibetan horns
and clouds of pungent smoke
I am a joyous child, doubtless
just like the old days

April, 2004
Dharamsala, India

The Upstairs Room

There is a room in my house
where a Rinpoche stays
when he comes to town that is
sometimes I wish he would leave
always I long for his return

He reads through texts as fast as the eye travels
    absorbing
    lightly
occasionally he will entertain my visitors
who kneel awkwardly, yet respectfully, before his bed
small talk is exchanged in a vast space filled
with photographs, a gallery of practitioners, old and young
a cell phone rings from under a frayed cushion
I am so jealous when he picks it up in mid-sentence
    undistracted
    curious
his mala softly clicks as it continues its course
Yes, there is pride in the room amidst the dreaming
    and *lungta,* a confidence of the ages

After dinner I put away the dishes
barefoot walk up the narrow stair
to find him sitting up, asleep
His finger rests alert to a place on the page
if I could read, it would point a way for me
    unconfused
    in the moment
comforted, I make a few minor adjustments to the shrine
backing away, I prostrate once alone
full of grief for the world
joyous that he inhabits my home

April, 2004
Gangtok, Sikkim

The Passerby

The ancient woman at the temple's foot
arranged in a hierarchy reminiscent
unavoidable on a woven mat worn
with a splash of red somewhere
a pail of base metal holds the last crumpled rupee
the mudra, one wizened dark hand
palm plaintiff, outstretched
in a pose of classical ease
the knee rising, not touching
beneath the hand
the remainder of her physique folded
into a collapsed tent of colored shawl

Yes, it is the same woman
provocative, not quite repulsive
positioned so deliberately
so that I argue with myself
anxious I might pass Vajrayogini by
or she may be the wife of the last taxi-driver
supplementing my last meager tip

Behind her, red monks in kora flow down the hill
prosperous at the seat of spiritual power
basking in the sun of exile
mumbling centuries of mantras
each one, one hundred eight times
they see her and walk by
they may have forgotten, if they ever did
how to look in her eye, regard the lines of her hand
pause with a word, a coin, even a touch
before they are gone
clockwise around the corner

Don't turn away!
All reflects through the lens of the passerby
who dares to gaze, not glance
not think, but discern

Don't turn away!
You are not an actor in a film shot in India
She is not someone else's life
a mere facile metaphor in a poem of India

Yes, she will die doubtless
as will you alone and penniless and
always too soon in some corner of the globe

Always too soon!
a thin knee pressing upwards
against the bedclothes
eyes questioning a passing caretaker
as your hand is routinely extended
in receipt of an evening narcotic

Her face, older than her age
younger than experience
Remember it from the past!
Now, she is your mother
Now, she is your child
in the city, of the farms
she arrives as the unconditioned gift
wizened at her birth
timeless in her paradox
of guilt and absolution
doubt and faith
of an averted gaze
or an encounter so sweet
to stir one ember of compassion
aglow in a heartless world.

October, 2002
Dharamsala, India

Protecting the Kingdom
I
The Border

One soldier
shabby uniform in place
World War I rifle at the ready
stares outward from the monastery
over the valley rended
by a waterless river bed
gray gravel strewn
all the way to Bengal

over his shoulder
the horizon lit by five stupas
built by a queen mother to honor
the limitless territory of the mind

not fully aware of what he protects
he has been born to this post
aligned to perfection
he is resolute, immoveable

behind him Dilgo Khentse
his body long since gone
teaches still precisely, cheerfully
into the dark age at the edge
of a protected kingdom.

II
The Checkpoint

A distance from the border
we come upon a checkpoint
Rinpoche seems asleep in the front seat
we fumble for carefully hidden passports

> expecting paperwork
> a soldier approaches
> epaulets brilliant in the drizzle

> crisp salute
> swooping bow
> hand covers mouth
> with uniform collar

> open face of the lama
> extended fingertips touch
> blessing

and we are waved, welcomed into the Kingdom.

III
Unbroken Lineage

In a hotel on the border of Bhutan
in the midst of a talk about something profound
Rinpoche laughs, mimics the Khampa pilgrims
journeyed on horse from Tibet to see His Holiness

He lies down grinning, his ear on his right elbow
slightly manic, alert, slovenly, yet knowing
and growls
"Well, Rinpoche!"
hoarse, husky
a voice from the ages
demanding the dharma
as his due

He becomes one
the unsullied mind
the untamed protector
riding a Tibetan steppe
beyond the crystal mountain
carrying a victory banner
etched on a depthless sky

and then the talk continues.

IV
Amrita

A sip of 35 rupee whiskey
purchased apprehensively
at the foot of the mountain
with a name like "Connoisseur's Choice"
from the feast shrine empowered
in the cave at Tak Sang
rendered intensely intoxicated
the lines of the sadhana
flowed off my tongue
I know intimately
every dimension of the space
and I begin to think
some magic is afoot
until I crack my skull
on that very same beam
as I stand up to leave.

V
Garuda

Emerge from the cave at Tak Sang
there is grief and romance in the air
eyes focus in the sudden change of light
a Black Eagle
broad and delicate fingered wings

Vivid
Warlike
Inscrutable

stoops meteoric across the sun
where form and shadow meet
rise over the waterfall
draw the eye skyward
a black diamond slices
through a sapphire sky

Disinterested
Ominous
Seductive

We, you are so present
there is no need for a sign
of hope for the dark age
nor for a footnote
to the inexplicable

second glance and he is gone
an imprint of a bird
on the mind.

April, 2004
Paro, Bhutan

La Transhumance de Vallée d'Ossau

In a village in a valley of the Pyrenees
summer begins with a subtle warmth
in the mountain air
rivulets of snowmelt reach into the village
to vary one's habitual stride

for the rare tourist
it is bucolic and benign
sheltered in the palm of the mountains
no anticipation, no expectation
one can rest in place
change to the pace
of a different rhyme

our two-star hotel, paid in advance
we dine on a terrace at the edge of the town
a bottle of Bordeaux, country paté
a red napkin lies across beige cloth
anchored by white china
practice our French on the waiter
who has a cousin in New York

a luxurious complacency
set upon by rumors from below
discordant clop of hooves
syllables mumbled, shouted
louder up the curved lane
we rise reluctantly to meet the scene

jaunty angled berets bob above the wall
red-cheeked farmers lead monotone herds
the waiter explains:
"Marron, c'est Normandie; jaune, ici."
each, a dog to urge onward
a dog to protect
on their way to mountain pasture
to a season of revival and rebirth

chimes echo down on the breeze
alert us to the movement above
a line of lamps, transparent pilgrims
drawn up the trail into the night
past rock huts and buttercups
bristly juniper inedible
yet another shade of gray slate
upward watching the waterfall
overtake itself, skim down
the side of the Cirque

the whole village is on the move
we pay the reasonable bill
no lingering over dessert
for cheeses age in the shadow
while higher climes await
and we have had more than our fill

we too must leave for the mountain
with or without a guide
at dawn we will set out
take whatever route to allow us
to see to the other side
while the Bearded One, the Lammergeier
is in a most merciful glide

even as we return to our hotel
the days hasten
toward dusk
the short grasses yellow
into wisps
and evanescent solace
begins an inebriant smile.

July, 1998
Gavarnie, France

The Way to Campostella
Notre Dame du Bon Port

Des Purs Sommets
des Montagnes les plus ardues
dont il aimait
Les grandes horizons et les dangers
Il est parti vers les sommets eternelles
n'ayant pas connu dans la vie
L'ombre de la vallée

Poised on the meridian zero
beneath the hotel balcony
three white nuns' habits meet
behind seventeen buses form
chaotic metal rectangles on a pavement canvas

Endless chatter and fumes
mask another hundred
intrepid pilgrims
on the way to Campostella
the field of stars, and beyond

Once this far
nowhere to seek refuge
except the church
as little as it is lofty
in the morning gloom

Here begins and ends the way of honor
in a kiosk to wide-eyed longing
for a miracle to change
the course of all existence
a hundred candles flicker to life

A once brightly painted Madonna
leans into space over travelers
who press forward to touch her skirts
weak-kneed spirits wilting in the awful shadow
of the Cirque, specter of an insuperable step

In a journey for resigned and zealous
sick and vigorous alike
knowing they will arrive too late
the passage not the destination
becomes the goal

So speak the gravestones on the ridge
raised in the soil
of those who never left
who healed themselves
laid stone upon stone

Gave birth in the meadow
in the company of lambs
on quilted wildflowers
and heard heaven
in the toil of her bells

Mothers who in patient exultation
plunge the babe in the frigid flume
raise up their uncrowned child
await confirmation, an appearance
for generations to follow

July, 1998
Gavarnie, France

Meeting the Teacher
(for RTR)

On entering the Valley I become illiterate
re-encounter a mysterious field of gravity
in the blood-red hills, the saints, the path
an ascending wind-spiral whips the flags
    into repetitive prayers
under the Red-tail wing-tilt
rootless sage brush
a humble barren ranch house
there is a holiness in the clouds
and a familiar face from Tibet
a mother's son of mine
re-enchantment in the recognition
the all encompassing
the no-big-deal smile
of welcome liberates
    the bondage of time
    the prison of language.

The last time was in Sikkim wasn't it?
Yesterday and tomorrow at once.

This time I snap a picture.

November, 2003
Fairplay, Colorado

Standing Ovation
(for CTR)

Once again at the podium exposed
cradled in the heart of the lineage
my toe seeks a stable ledge
and after a precipitous pause
Naropa welcomes me back

somehow, sometime
there is a larger script that has held me
an unroped mountaineer
to the shoulder of the summit
applause fills my room wondrous

somewhere, somehow
if I could hear you applauding
but the silence is
    crystalline
    terrific

except someone is laughing uproariously
in the green room
or further away in Tibet
while planting a flag on the peak

I remain confused as to who is speaking
but never lose my voice
as a careful choice of words floats into
a grand beyond-language space

Just when I understood letting go
I care so much
Just when it meant so much
I loosed my grasp
into an avalanche of blessings.

November, 2003
Boulder, Colorado

Not So, Just So

I'm looking for the face I had before the world was made.

William Butler Yeats

White Pelican

The telescope probes into the weak sundown
The winter aloneness is complete

I find you amidst a thousand Ringed-bills
statuesque, out of place and time

massive golden bill hidden in a shawl of snow
White Pelican stands asleep on the January ice.

I can't help myself
I rush to Whole Foods
buy you mercury-free halibut
and a stuffed juvenile pelican from Toys R Us
soon we fly to Trinidad together
into balmy evenings and Scarlet Ibis sunsets
I travel economy but upgrade you to first class
drinking rum, a garland of hibiscus round
    your eccentric head
cocking your sword-like beak
at an enchanted attendant
who allows you to fly
all the way without a seatbelt
I am relieved of your plight
intoxicated by your charms

The Pelican remains unmoving
still on sturdy yellow legs

soft feathers on the shoulder
ruffle in the evening chill.

January 12, 2004
Valmont Reservoir
Boulder, Colorado

Not So, Just So

I

Drawn toward you mother of all
Life as it was
Life as it will be
History and prophesy confused
The search is intensified, prolonged
What do we know?
Do we make a difference?
Gandhi, Mountbatten fade in the dust
We are alike in the struggle
Unique in the dream
Thousands line the roadside, waiting
An indistinguishable brown movement
    on the surface of the earth
Background of white and green, purity and karma
    perfect as it is.

II

Along the Ganges a mogul garden sublime
bejeweled walls untouched by centuries
    of riparian litter
await the monsoon
to be washed clean and away
    the sacred, the profane
    the elegance, the squalor

Gone too are distinctions of the intellect
in a land where faith comes so easily
    instantly
    intuitive

In the courtyard, saddhu and bureaucrat struggle
to organize a world long since lost to chaos
    irretrievable
    memorable
enlivened by tiger, diving falconet and the peafowl's cry
    anguish
    agony

On the riverbank, flood waters
never extinguish the pyres
for humanity's fuel is inexhaustible

Within the walls stand numberless
waiters with nothing to do
like actors with no lines to say
for whom the cue never comes
but to serve another indigestible course
    in an endless banquet
credit cards are not accepted
your currency never exchanged.

III

Flat tire along a steamy street of stalls
beneath the golden-pink sunset over Katchendzonga
three-legged dogs speak of unseen suffering
rhododendron blossom explodes
over the misty gompa
    the kindness, the humor
    the callousness, the resignation
a deer repeats its bark
at the tiger's relentless approach
the fifth-generation elephant driver rejoices
at the 200 rupee tip for a tiger sighting
no one mourns
the endless passage
of forgotten species

Dawn arrives new, crisp
over the Corbett plain
pushing the haze ahead of it
the shopkeeper waters down his dusty stoop
youthful monk voices sing the morning chants
while the Hindu driver bows at a passing shrine
its whites and reds strike through the roiling
    of humanity awakened
a child bathes with a water buffalo in a muddy pool
lapwings exult on the shore

A truck laden with desperate chickens
takes to the road through a ray
of sunlight as it filters down
    on the shuttered Mahakala
a pilgrim stands tall facing the east
to prostrate to the unseen
the mother's son cleans his automatic rifle
at the border post
an elegant woman in green and purple silk
a mere shimmer of sari stands erect
adjusts the sling for her child
and moves off in search of firewood.

IV

I am indebted
I am redeemed
back in Boulder
In a life believed to be mine
Exclusive orderly meaningful
In a shaken construct revived
I had persuaded myself that I was
Headed somewhere
Had accomplished
Will be remembered
Would live to die in dignity
in some familiar way
surrounded by the familiar
Not so
Just so.

Cultural Paranoia

Why is it not one person in India has change for a 100 rupee note?

Why are all those men staring at me?

Why can't I get one out of 500 million women to look at me?

You paid 30 rupees for a taxi to the temple?

No, sahib, it is not at all spicy.

My, the salad looks so good.

Why do the monks all have cell phones?

Why do they have those fancy treaded footrests in the toilets?

Why does not one shop owner paint his storefront a bright clean color?

Why do the Red Jungle Fowl keep crossing the road?

Why didn't that girl wave back?

What lepers?

April, 2004
Dharamsala to Delhi, India

India Through a Car Window
I
Birth

Out of a million street-front shops leaps
a single silhouette vivid against the dark pall
the crush of indescribable contents

a resonance from my stomach out to his clasped fingers
as my eyes struggle to adjust to his light
a barber nonchalant sits in his own chair

awaiting the birth of a fifth child somewhere
I lose sight of him instantly, our futures part
forever in the dust, the fumes of chaos

II
Livelihood

Upon a trodden path
Bundled kindling floats above
Violet gold shimmering

Silken red shoulders
Bend amidst eager rice stalks
One less hungry child

Water buffalo bath
Thin brown arms splash the river
Disappointed flies

III
Karma

A vast chasm of separation
until a great cellular coincidence
no, a collision joins

one man, not just any man
aligned by the law of the roadside
missed by inches

by the careening car
in which I sit looking into his eyes
as if I have known him forever.

What engine
wills it to decide
the fate of two of one billion?

March, 2004
Delhi to Nainital, India

The Tourist in Room 106

unshaven
motley and vague
ambling along
trousers drooping over hips
on a crowded jetty of jumbled slabs
a tern slices low across
my imagination
falls open overripe
grateful
to a Mediterranean village
name unknown, whose
beach-teeming
background of carnival
riotous sound incomprehensible
table cloths juxtaposed behind
inconceivable body shapes
articulate a collage of life's punch lines
pause for the fisherman's back cast
in mid-step
a tremendous chromium lure
arches the graphite rod
across a half-reveal of uninhibited belly
I inhale to cast a youthful silhouette onto the granite
good for another hundred meters
past the hawkers'
gallery of tawdry prizes
to the laughable security of the hotel lobby

July, 1998
Miramar Hotel
Valras Plage, France

Lake Elementeita Seduction

> *I long to write a poem of Africa always as it was*
> *except it does not reveal a time to me*
> *when the mirror displays it true and pure.*

In the Rift Valley again
a man shoulders a telescope
and with a mimicry of walk,
starts out
willing to be shocked.

I am fearless in a blinding sunset
over the Western escarpment
looking down and away
attracted to a conversation among the cowbells.
There, two thin giants meet, growing
Masai stalked tall out of the ground
undeniable black cloaked red-orange,
and the depthless eyes of the land open.
    seductive
    uncaring.
They lift their eyes up without humility
raise sculptured hands
magnetic, an understanding
evokes a wave like no other
    eye from eye
    black on white
    wisdom to intellect
connect in a recognition of no history
and I anonymous enter
a landscape beyond the mirror
and Kenya is there
only a wave away.

I can see forever.
Over and beyond necked-scarred cattle
slaking the thirst of the Masai for centuries
    endured
    entwined
Crowned Plovers proud over skeletal legs
not feeding, flushed by my stride
with strident call they resettle on the emaciated land.
A single gazelle postured among sparse bush
alert, juxtaposed with goat herd
urged forward by boy's inherited bird-voice skill.
Exposed Spurfowl dart, retreat into thorn bush
granting turquoise lizards another day
on the blood-clay-burned skin of Africa.

Walking so slowly, gaining strength
an ambition to comprehend all
I can see forever
from Lord Cole's phallus-tomb
of conquest, into defeat
on porch, from plane, from bareback
astride the land
    broken
    satiated.
While again and again over Lake Elementeita,
white pelicans tainted with pink hues
spiral to altitude, unbound
compounds reforming a mysterious alchemy
in the vaporous shroud over the land.

The land awaits only a wave away.
Many Africas in mind's mirror reflected
acacia trees flattened out
umbrella'd over grasslands
dotted with silhouette of ostrich
sloping hills woven down to stream beds

where leopards wait for dusk
in limbs of rainy season trees
vultures adorn leafless trunks
    cloaked
    patient
the hideous grace of a will to wait forever
over a track of skeletons of wildebeest
conjured beasts, invisible snakes
and elephant waltz-walk
delicate, unharming miracle of evolution
giraffe with brain weightless above the trees.
There is no future only past,
a timetable of arrivals and departures
as I walk seeing
forever without prediction.

A wave away, a bomb explodes in Nairobi.
The face of one Africa turns
to catch the slanting, failing light.
In shadow pictures a human realm flickers
Arab dhows leaving the coast for Zanzibar markets
laden with slaves packed in the 24-inch 'tweendecks,
the distracted slaughter of Bugandan chiefs
idle executions repeated nightmare
of human barter, plunder
as hills of elephant tusks rise nearby
the infectious malarial slime
    unyielding
    unveils
to the monstrous ego of the educated
the Africa of Burton
of Stanley, of Speke and on and on
in hollow-cheeked wandering
in search of the Source
reckless with any truth
wreaking memory's vengeance

on those with no history.
They build false horses on a castleless savannah
taken in by the resilience of the land
that casts them aside misunderstood
    uncivilized
    demented
Yet, resisting all rescue
living on occasional allegations of reality
destined to die in a tent
blood and mud staining
what was believed an ultimate history
in diary pages scattered.

And now a bomb explodes in Nairobi
sensed by Gerenuks born in a Chicago zoo
behind stores of leopard coats and zebra rugs
echoes of Arab markets, a life for a trinket
and the bloodied face of a Finance Minister
another father and son
two generations tending the white man's outpost
    expunged
    absorbed
 in the relentless pulse beat of the land.

On the edge of the escarpment I have seen forever
for this prehistoric rift in the land awaits unthinking
only a wave away.
And I am risen again, reborn
from the alkaline slime
tinctured with a volcanic spume
the perfect pH arrives, unsuspected
by the roaming beasts watching
as I lower my hand.

August 7, 1998
Masai Mara, Kenya

Cote d'Azur Vertigo

It is a place where dreams sing out loud.
A light peculiar searches out the soul.
Memory surfaces as warmth
on the skin perspires, flushes the face.

I stand at the edge of an incipient spell
a nausea of expectancy
the discontent of memory
below me
a cliff faces into the blue
of a precipitous sky and water
decorated by Roman arches
that hold The Grand Corniche
at the head of a narrowing cove
where the sea magnifies
the bottom as it shallows
to a mottled pebbled beach

a collage of houses waits
mustard walls and blue shutters
sloped maroon tile roofs
interrupt angled lanes
scattered umbrellas
white tablecloths behind Cypress trees
waiters in black vests ply the patio
wait upon the earthen skin of green-eyed women
too distant for precision
yet with imagination everywhere
the eye sees vividly
and a past abides in the landscape
as kindling for the present

enveloped in the liquid sapphire air
the sensual purity of the instant
often cues regret
the shadow of lost opportunity
missed encounters, books unread
stifled conversations, imagined liaisons
a crossing of endless choices.

Here
all is tea with a slice of lemon
    a spoon of honey
their faces in the sunlight innocent and brave
as they moved me then, they move me now
how they talked and drank
and danced before they died

they paced and smoked and argued
over Success and Duty and Neglect
occasionally to plunge
into Love and Passion
and Reckless Choices
without Consequence

Then
no awareness of the meter
the line breaks of our lives
if we had only known
how rare and sensitive
the alchemy
the erosion down
from the rawest of material
into skeletal
dust or diamond
a new-found element
the jewel, the pith instruction
to light a life

Now
all is gin, sweet vermouth
    a splash of campari
    and a twisted lemon
the shaker frosted over the marble bar
white-gloved hand
pours rose nectar
into a fluted glass
for I am
handsome in their recollection
restless in their anticipation
youthful heir to their vigor
Far Better For their Memory

Long
they are gone entr'acte
to travel with other theatres
leaving me the anguish, the delight
of memory and imagination
Dizzy
Drunk with Missing
pierced by an angle of sunlight
through an hidden barometric zone
one could paint
write forever
without food or drink
or merely remember for

The sea is a sacrament.
The land sustenance.
All is illuminated
by the eccentric
cant of the sun.

July, 1998
St Jean Cap Ferrat, France

A Visit to the Chatterwood Home at Middle Chagrin

We had not called ahead for directions
we drive on the left, mostly
as innocent tourists might
follow our progress closely on a map
late and lost, we close on a village
called Middle Chagrin, whence spread out
many colors of way, below numbers
that express a unconvincing measure of the miles

We pull up in a circular courtyard
empty of cars, no longer a manor house
betrayed by the electronic lock
and retrofitted air conditioners
bird feeders half-filled
reveal the only sign of care

Following a careless wave, we enter a room
confront a line-up of eligible victims
who gesticulate wildly in disjointed
jawing with invisible relatives
whose ghostly signatures we witnessed
in the cheap flowered guest book in the hall

Staggered by the desperate recognition
    of an aging
we loom over fifteen middle-class women
their backs to the wall in the drawing room
    as they drool dying
in the pantry, caretakers gossip
personalities extinguish in the drawing room

She chairbound, us kneeling
close to her shallow breath
veined, twitching transparency of a palm

grasps my wrist and gives it all away in a word
    "It's a disaster."
she whispers an absolute, a summation
    "It's a disaster."
no argument can be found

I yearn to halt the orbit
the evolution, of this twirling planet
memorize the Compleat Works of Yeats
Newton, all of them
freeze all wisdom
evolution in its tracks
enshrine a romantic landscape
in unfading oils
for, too painful to confront decay
we are left to worship
at the altar of ongoingness of all

Rooted in an interminable moment
unable to flee
we linger over a nuthatch
reflected through a darkening glass
on a now empty feeder

We make good our escape
some instinctual echo
prompts us to check the petrol
that rests at empty, fortunate
for I prefer the narrow yellow roads
hedges tall protective on both sides
that meander without objective
through the country
and avoid the fast and direct
and then, when I arrive
I am even more surprised.

July, 1998
Alresford
Hampshire, England

La Dordogne

All is tame
a canvas of ochre random stones
misshapen hewn into locking puzzle
rust roof lines against round olive hills
smoothed by centuries of eyes eroding
pens of resigned plump ducks of Perigord
a woven basket displays miniature clamshells
a perfect harvest
wild trees pruned
placed
and shaped
over Bergerac and chevre picnic beside still
white-lined tarmac almost glossy
bridges nearby a languid mill stream there comfortable trout
waltz a lazy hide-and-seek among green reed streamers
suspended over sculptured tan limestone
where cave paintings lie hidden
even a dipper appears
arranged on a ripe onyx rock and
echoes the bemused black-tied maître d'hotel
all is dressed
delicious disguised

a good place to start a dharma center.

Toul Sleng – The Hill of the Poisoned Trees

Through the gap over the sill, more than a draught, an ominous wind evacuates the space. He has no choice but to open the door, aware that the source consumes all, not that day, that singular minute, but eternally. He shudders, an icy undertow around the ankle bones, reverberates up the skeleton to the inner ear as an invited dizziness, the disorientation of freedom.

The door hisses, folds open
a few easy steps off the bus
and I am standing in the dust
the sun is brilliant
the air tumid, peculiar
stultifies the mind and warns

a path convolutes across twisted metal, crumbled concrete
Where does the tour begin?
someone pays my admission
the guide disappears
no wide-eyed children offer to lead me to a unique corner
I am separated, estranged yet still
unwilling to be taken by surprise

I enter the first room or the last room – who knows?
If they told me I could not believe them.
rusted cot, ammo box toilet, pipe with shackles
a wire mattress, red-brown and dull
reflects up at me viciously
atop tiles played upon by schoolchildren
now a final chessboard inexorable with no rules

a voice whispers
Go back to the bus.
the guidebook had mentioned offhandedly
Look for the bloodstains.
I don't have to

writhe deeper in barbwire
in desperation and delight
    of being alive
    of not being one of them
    in the delusion of a separate life
Label it aberrant insanity, now! Please!
caught by the dread, the gray adhesive walls
    of unquestioned dullness
    of the certainty of habit
    the indifference
    of no difference

I read the scrawls
hear a sigh within my own breast
the last testament of the literate
    of the doctor
    the teacher
    nun and monk
    historian and the translator
they are all gone now
drowned in fear subsumed by the soil
a transmission broken up by static in a storm of Year Zero

the panic of what if
there is no one who remembers
    an alphabet, times table
    a conjugation of past, present and future
    or an elementary catechism
    the secret dimensions of Angkor
    and trust in a tale told by the bank of the Mekong
To tell the truth you need not remember anything.
what if no one remembers the question

my teachers' eyes dim
my recollection ebbs
    of a cultured life
    truth and beauty
    of an elegant grandfather on a manicured lawn
    a bequest of harmony for my blond grandchildren
for the astonishment of a human birth

out into the hall, another door, then another
endless corridors leading nowhere to the same endpoint
Don't tell me it has always been this way!
a collage of the stains of agony
most of all the soft cries against the darkness
adrift on a river of unquenched suffering
    it is my time
    no their time
If you confess, it will all be over.
up on the screen the projection of a world awry
the pounding metronome of a careless heart
a slow turning of the ineffectiveness of good
the hopelessness of blame

I listen catatonic to the cries
    of schoolchildren
    their teachers scolding
    their parents calling
lost to the high-pitched commands of the twelve-year old guards
now a crescendo, a wailing of the unheard
cell upon cell, bricks and mortar laid from the inside out
Nous pouvons construire à la liberté un temple
ou un tombeau des mêmes pierres.
past rooms for VIP's then ordinary folk as you or me
up the stairs to the children's rooms
desperate for it to end

into a gallery of the victims and captors staring
all eyes are on me haunted on the spot
by uncomprehending blank spaces
dare to return the look
face the contagion
oil paintings shimmer in the fluorescence
crude brushwork of the most refined inhumanity

the room empties
solitude envelopes across the cracking concrete
bile rises in the throat
empathy has turned to hysteria
there is a triple beat to my heart
    Where am I?
    Where was I?
I do not recognize the way out
I am one of them, they are part of me
I offer up my genitals, my fingernails
I confess my disobedience
hope of rescue bleeds away
there opens a abyss
    of right and wrong
     relative or the absolute
     prisoner and torturer
     light and dark
wisdom and insanity lie indistinguishable
vengeance and forgiveness inadequate

I am unsteady
    reach out a hand
    touch the wall
so cold, my hand is bloodless
    reel out into the hall
    down the stairs
    under the gallows
    tumble the skulls

a ridge of skeletons stretches away under a merciless sun
hurry past hasty graves toward an apparent break in the wire
a beggar turns away
at the edge a Magpie Robin scratches amidst the shards
a smiling child tries to sell me a postcard
    I had a dollar left
    it is gone now

the bus is pink and air-conditioned
most of the group is shopping
I have forgotten the meeting time
Where is Bayard? She has been in there too long.
Yet I cannot will myself to re-enter
    there
    is no
    there
    to seek refuge

I stand on my heels in a meager slice of shade
    cast by a strangely healthy tree
anger floods through me
    Pol Pot has died in his sleep
    Duch languishes unindicted
    the UN, the USA, the CIA
move on to other paranoid entanglements
all are unrepentant yet protected
by the sheer incredulity of the bystander
the implication of the witnesses
a history that can only be read as fiction

I could suffocate in the ambiguity
    enshrine the horror
    now tear down the prison
    photograph everything
    now expunge the record
    stand them in the dock
    then abrogate the law
a collective amnesia insures that nothing happens

an outbreath constricted down deep
    by a murderous notion
    a confusion immeasurable
I cross a black hole of ideology
my compass swings wildly
Someone tell me the difference between right and wrong!
I have to understand
but what if there is no answer
what is the point?
    to do no harm
    not to confuse
    to return to the bus
    to take to the street
I have come too far not to be involved
there is no returning home
    until then
each moment is a choice.

March, 2006
Phnom Penh, Cambodia

My Window On the Atlantic

To see a wren in a bush, call it 'wren' and go on is to have seen nothing. To see a bird and stop, watch, feel, forget yourself a moment, be in the bushy shadows, maybe then feel 'wren'— that is to have joined in a larger moment, with the world.

Chögyam Trungpa, Rinpoche

Wales: A Glimpse at a Time
I
Gwynedd Genetics

The play of light upon the land
the sound of an accent behind the ruin
the way the sheep huddle among boulders jumbled
the raw perfection of the cliff as it meets the sea
Gwynedd becomes me

like an ancestral amulet lost in the lining
of a once-worn father's jacket
resurrected from a missing-key cellar trunk
mildewed for generations
all along I have sensed it silently

there is no album of yellowed photos
no genealogical exhibits and margin notes
no map with penciled circles
or postcard from a cousin
and whimsy is an insufficient summons

with a surprised suddenness
when on a sabbatical from habit
my thumb reclaims, revives
the shape neglected, a skeletal fossil thaws
after a bitters in the beamed pub

my arteries pulse, cheeks flush
I am, tongue unleashed
transported
an amnesiac in Wales
I assume it has always been this way.

II
Skomer Island Elemental

We walk face down in the wind
to follow the tracks of slugs
our antennae probe the gale outward
past farmyard rubble where stooped grasses
and a few sheep seek solace together

the rain presses upward from the sole
to bead through my beard
a ruddy Irish seawater immersion
salty and sweet, a primordial pH
unaccustomed toes learn to brace in the wind

drawn outward by the soaring joy
of Fulmar, the energetic flight of the Murre
with a nonchalance of the ages
they land to feed their young below
on the sheer cliff clinging to a telescope lens

held transfixed by a Peregrine stare
fierce with a peculiar vigor undaunted
sourceless lightning flashes approach
I cast a backward glance at a backlit
Sarcen luminous, perhaps ominous on the knoll

precisely where it is expected
then a hurried amble
mimic the confidence of Nature
willing my companion forward
back to shelter and a bird book.

III
Skomer Island Evolution

The little ferry docks in rough Irish seas
at the base of a cliff, glistening black
we disembark gingerly, watching each step
at eye level stage left stand five Razorbills
dignified aloof and certainly unafraid
their strange bills appear perfect in the spume
this line-up of Auks smart on a rock shelf
framed diagonally by the encrusted gangplank
perhaps the household staff
in formal dress for my arrival, or
a stag line content to observe
flaunt their bills with an attitude
"you've never seen one like this before"
divert my attention from the peril at hand
a disguised order, a comic hierarchy
amid a world that tries to throw me off
the horizontal rain, the surf arrives
argues with itself returning
the torque and plunge of the rail
first the barnacles, a deceptive traction
then green seaweed, nature's teflon
covers every level foothold
I am enthralled, gain equilibrium
begin to strut up the gangplank
yet they pay me no attention

admittedly trite, yet there is so much to see
and, we believe, little time this life
so many elegant distinctions from Kittiwake to Fulmar
aeons of subtle refinement etched
as if for my enjoyment
the timeless artistry of silken feathers
hues of grey mantle
of bill and eye and hood

Nature disguises sacrifice with beauty
such struggle in their Grace
for betrayed to my heart's eye
a mountain of skeletons rises bleached upward
since creation toward the sun
that tells the story of Shearwaters entwined
embraced in a dance with slate-hearted gulls
who wait all night unthinking
circling evolution's gauntlet
for the next young Shearwater's flightless scurry
between burrow and cliff edge
full of my hopes, my dreams
to launch into a new dawn.

IV
Another Narrow Escape

Perched precarious in the rear of a caravan
from an accepting rattan chair
my eyes claim the coast of Wales

crested waves blown slanting onto the sand
shape, repeat below in a moment
to a mist-heat horizon of my castle

its grayish roofs oddly intersecting
a forgotten farmstead of sheep and thistle
obsolete tractor mostly rust

nearby a farmer's child on stunted horse
my spire and abandoned abbey
over fields of stone-walled squares

past my inelegant publick house
silver and green petrol pumps
a coast road moves thinly out of sight

carrying the teenage driven jaguar
that nearly killed us again
returning from the bliss of Skomer.

V
Pentre Ifan Tinnitus

A simple car park
a space awaits
over a rickety stile
a short mud path through gorse
where a sparrow eludes

out to a broad meadow
on the side of gentle ridge
not mowed not overgrown
a patchwork of fields falls away
into the Nevern Valley

where, precisely in ancient Wales
placed five millennia ago
stands an altar arranged
a tomb for a princess
exudes a confident geomancy

a humbleness of perfection
on the shoulder of the summit
no need to usurp the ridge
a feat of engineering, yet
the arrangement appears random

not crude, nor barbaric
the sophistication is hidden
an order surprises, coalesces
my pace becomes ceremonial
not somber, but uplifted

now, the warrior's horizon is hemmed
    by paint-branded sheep
haphazard stone-wrought walls imprison
    spiritless cultivation

the guidebook is ignored
for looking away is reckless
a capstone of sixteen tons
somehow placed delicately on a tripod of three
step through, under at your peril, Oh Prince

your time may have come
the mystery to be revealed
to eyes veiled by the opacity of intellect
here, from nowhere descends
a bequest, a request
for a revivified embrace of nature

I sip coke from an aluminum can
raise a lightening rod, no, a toast
to the majesty of timeless questions
as an aural why incessant, insistent
    rings in my ears

too civilized, answerless, I am infused
with an overwhelming urge to bow
I bend, venerate
but before tourists, I pretend
to pick up some litter.

VI
Snowdon Mindscape

Identical, no indistinguishable
warblers ring changes
over a village
typical in North Wales

the clients in the hotel restaurant
appear born there
by a river of dappled-white stone
with trout and wagtail, no dippers yet

from a store built of ancient stone
with used leather volumes
unruly elders issue across the green
onto the vacated rail bed

to walk untrainable dogs
passing with a loving unintelligible greeting
I suspect reports no improvement
in the weather

on mist green-walled scree slopes
orderly tonsured sheep forage gently
I impose Gainsborough on the harsh
landscape of gorse prickle and uneroded granite

storm clouds hurtle upwards
darkening, after Turner
with his passionate brush
a romance of stroke against the grain

artistry after Wordsworth, weaving
a lacework of words
of optimism amid the ruins
of the mill site long abandoned

its keyless locks and rusted wheels
never really to capture it
you too must embrace and leave
it all behind to time

so relax about a next word
your net worth or the exchange rate
you are so fortunate
simply awed
waiting for insight
no, a next breath, in Wales.

My Window on the Atlantic

Writing is not a contract made with phenomena
    a pleasing arrangement with Nature
I have nothing to say and cannot admit it
    All the words spoken.
      The metaphors exhausted.
Yet the Sea will not let me alone

Of course my mind is a match for reality.
Over a pellucid sea
    a simulacrum of Gannets
    and life becomes a poem.
Paris in the thirties, a mere dream
    the rough smoke of a Gauloise
    mixes with the heat
    of l'Absinthe
    going down
the regret is palpable

Pause to recollect the birds I may never see.
    Vireos have fled south.
    Leaves stripped from the branch.
"yet" and the "if only" waft suspended in the air
hopelessness is not mourning the cycle
    looking forward to the next moment
    a delicious corruption

I had arisen in the morning in all my glory
in my superior over-educated maleness
to wield the pen as a sword
then to gaze out my window on the Atlantic
    Twenty-knot wind
    Five-foot waves
    Frozen spume

the unedited chaos of nature
where a male Harlequin Duck
each painted feather in place
rides the winter surf
with ease and decorum
    off the tumbled granite
    with his harem of twenty females

Who is cast in God's image here?
My morning hierarchy is reordered.

Beyond, a Gannet feeds herself
    plunges again and again
    accurate arrow emerges
    pierces the Nor'easter
This requires a sense of humor
she generously lends to me
just when I was getting serious
about my writing.

Fall Clouds Over Ipswich Bay

Life's taught me
how not to write haiku
unlearn it you fool

Passion for life
inverse proportion
to do list

Double-crested, European
Who-knows Cormorant
all identified

Not know
miss entirely
full eclipse

Atlantic churn
full moon over Italy
custard and butter to my window

Lesser, Greater
shades of gray mantle
gulls and green tea

As white space in water color
divine and blank
I sit down to write

Ancestor worship
when you place the family portraits
in storage, lovingly

Wherever I stay
a closet-full of polished
shoes appears

Parts of the ocean distinguish
just look at a wave
over here now

What if, my memory
holds my whole life together
no haiku

When young tanager
sees September snow
fly into thin air fearless

Soldier martyr mothers daughters
shed the tears
of the god of Abraham

I need a new battery
for my applause meter
But Ho

It seems perfectly natural
for grandson to be fearful
of my mustache
But Oh

Past the loyal buoy
lie five spider-like trawlers
killing fields for jobs and families

Georges' Banks –
Bush and Soros
down by the corral
glare circling

Feel the discomfit
avuncular gaze
frustrated muse

The Point is
all about
haulabout
not halibut

Adjectives

Up early waiting on the electrician
the day too fresh for judgment

Soaked in a morning rain
the sea is leaden, restless

Horizon empty under weighted clouds
my window frames the display

Awkward cartwheels of Gannets fishing
a convention of Black-backs observe them, jealous

Loons cross diagonally as skybound arrows
penetrate the space of my mind

Two harbor seals off the point circle a lone lobster pot
they play as if the rules were random but clear

Purple Sandpipers stalk the kelp
in desperation or enthusiasm, I cannot tell

Adjectives arise and fall lightly
these vivid projections seem uncensored

Yet unwilling or unable to let alone
nature is sculpted by the mind

Doubtlessness falls before pride, sensing
if I went out the wind-howl would strip my mind bare.

Shanghai'd Mind

Haulabout House from the safety of my sofa
first September morn way past dawn
Eastern sun confronts my drowsiness
I fumble for my list, one hand holds steeped green tea
glance over the ocean, empty to a lazy eye

But See! The schooner three-masted under full sail
black hull defiant scarred by the waves
enters between thin mists
sentinels for the bank of a following fog
within its varnished cabins a wanderlust abides

overhead the incessant creak of rigging
backlit crew move at random on a rope-cluttered deck
a line of opaque potholes hides a ruthless story
to disappear on the wake of nostalgia
in a moment, a horn wails from the fog

I am swept willingly over the waves of Cape Horn
to the albatross islands, the ports of the orient
I live amidst warriors and thieves
dance with princesses and whores
in the brilliance and among the sordid
amid depthless wisdom and ecstasy limitless
touched by fire and fear, riches unbounded
and the deepest loneliness I have known

until someone enters the room
romantic poet tossed aside, panting
depleted in the corner
of the Pier One sofa.

September, 2003
Halibut Point
Rockport, Massachusetts

a/k/a

Oh, exquisite one preening off the point
white face radiant, innocent
silent in the New England sea
a coincidence of particles
of light, rides the surf
a tapestry of sub-atomic spaces
the absolute sprung to my eye
huntress of the waves, the deep
abides, awaits the call
the subtle warming of the north

sight delicious surrenders
binoculars focus unwilled
the sixth sense rises jealous
to ravage mystery in her bed
gasps, yes, it was
an animal
a bird, a duck

family genus
species gender
plumage winter
all is ordered
back to my tea
and an editorial
wait now
there is opinion
emotion, even anger
carried in the name

why are we so quick
to label the things we love
the name moves faster
than the eye of the heart
the magic of the formless
unspeakable to behold
the wild, the inexplicable
ensnared, explained
in a single thought

the world becomes
a galaxy of adjectives
love, a barren noun
sacred beauty
a recitation of field marks
awareness, an argument
over what I have seen

granted her male is Long-tailed
the gift of communication
is her signature
she crests the foam again
cries out and wins me back.

When the elegant
long-trained gown-wearing
Countess Canard appears
at the spring edge of the ice
she is addressed Oldsquaw
Eskimo women straighten erect

Men go out in search of seal
as they have always done
just as the ice is breaking
onto frigid flows
at the edge of subsistence
they pause
as they have often done
to listen to the Oldsquaws
catch them in the midst
join those private conversations
they can't have with their wives

of gossip and wisdom
centuries of patient observation
of freezes and the thaws
tides and eclipses
and to bear jokes lightly
up from the south
on the Mic Mac's, Narragansett's
and more recently, the Pilgrims
never known for their humor

And when the women
complete the final chores
shed layers of worldly calluses
to emerge chrysalis like
as they have always done
they go with the Oldsquaw
and fly to Paradise
the liberation
of no label.

November, 2006
Boulder, Colorado

Winter Waves Off Halibut Point

When the electrician comes
every appliance
runs like new

Wrathful Manjushri
obliterates all memory
of rupas

Golden sliver of marmalade
offers up
empty plate

White-winged Scoters
crest casually
that Portugal wave

Sun
Rain
Appreciation beyond words

A painter friend sells
Italian landscapes
by the square inch

A flash of lightening
lights a blossom
love, war
and you are on your deathbed

Vast is the robe of liberation
I
reckons
and opts for a
crumpled handkerchief

You cannot steal
the treasury
of dharma

Late evening atlas
appalled by the play of armies
timeless over the globe
preceded by pictures of the cranial fossils
    of an evolving hominid

I am somewhat convinced
birds fly by the window
even when I am not watching

Today, Thursday
appears to be
for the Gannet
a flying day

They could just fool me
and go through the motions
But No

am I pretentious
when all of phenomena
genuine

Winter's wave on granite
Catsbriar last leaf shudder
suspiciously nonchalant

Twenty knot wind
freezing crystal mist
sloop under reefed sail
plunges toward Nova Scotia
arteries pulse
synchronous
in my arm chair

Old men in drab windbreakers
joust at Dunkin' Donuts
like Harlequins in the ice-froth
    of Hoophole Cove
poetic license

Hypochondria
at fifty-nine
every blemish
becomes life-threatening
the way it was at nineteen

Tell me now honestly
what is my greatest fear
as the next wave
pauses before it breaks

Every cell of my body
recoils at the thought
of lighting a large fire
brewing a pot of green tea
and
all day
sitting with or without
pen and paper
wouldn't people find out?

A related thought:
Neruda arises simultaneously
inspired
not even depressed
and
pen poised too
encounters the same self

Just now
my desire to review
the morning's work
stopped intuition in her track
popped creativity's balloon
the muse departs

Furrows into the autumn sun
Rusted out tractor
Dreams under the elm

November 20, 2003
Halibut Point, Massachusetts

Frontier Stories

Go west, young man, and grow up with the country.

John B. L. Soule

Appointment with the Assessor

Halfway to Saguache driving due west
    to record papers
    reduce the tax
    consolidate my holdings
morning sun slants over the Needles
pale grasses intersperse the night's snow
reflects off the San Juan peaks
like the interior of a crystal hemisphere
the Valley luminous from the four directions

my eyes strain to encounter the light
on one of numberless stringed poles
silhouette etched in the darkest of brown
golden-streaked hood or helmet
monk or royalty I cannot distinguish
magnificent countenance
talons clasp the high voltage line
immoveable, crackling
in anticipation of flames
emanates a searing benevolence

enthroned
in the valley center
skewered
in the glower of no expectation
muscles slacken like prey
relax into a clairvoyance
    of no past
    no future
decelerating snow tires chant in unison
    immediate death
    absolute me
    immediate death
    absolute me

I am overtaken under the dome
devoured in the embrace
in the valley of exquisite illusion
as it floats upon an ancient sea

the rustle of shoulder feathers
sends gusts down the valley
    sways barbed wire
    sweeps tumbleweed into its wake
prairie dogs stand on hind paws
their eyes black, tiny and fierce
transfixed as I
too far from our burrows
my exhale goes with it
over an arrhythmic heart

no, this is not the road to Damascus
    no recollecting one's self
nor a mistaken apparition
    no getting over it
no thought of flight
regal eyes follow me
I drive on devoured

in the basement of the courthouse
the clerk has lived all her life in this valley
she sifts through pages of maps that render predictable
a tenuous claim to the land
    Has she seen?
    Dare I inquire?
my heart reaches out to her, not in sympathy
but for all that we have been through together
battered cabinets with penciled labels A-Z
obsolete Selectric in the shadow of manufactured light
ashtray hidden in the metal drawer
an interrupted lunch of Pepsi and fries

she unrolls the survey and confirms
    the location of my lots
    calculates the tax and fees
    takes my check in silence
and stamps and signs each page in a stack
she gives me instructions
hands me the papers
as she has done a thousand times before

but with a tenderness that surprises
I return to Crestone and look for him
lonely I drive directly
into the domain of His Majesty
where the cringing profile of the dreaming Pica
    carries his soaring lesson
where the winged seer of awareness
    leaves a shadow
    across the face of Kit Carson.

October, 2004
San Luis Valley, Colorado

Walk Up French Joe Canyon

Already it is early morning
miles from anywhere
about three miles to go
I work up the narrow arroyo
strewn with brush and boulders
long dried puddles, baked run-off sand
head-clearing dry sun argues with anxiety
over a miscalculation of water
or gout that may cripple
short of the goal: the Rufous-capped Warbler
a rarity I have come to see

along the way, so much delight
Black-chinned Sparrow singing
a Dusky-capped Flycatcher
field marks so clear
a Beryline Hummer surprises
darts over flowers
well out of its range

then a persistent wrenlike scratching
lower down in the brush beside the trail
unusual, curious, I was drawn closer
still unidentified, tantalized by a nature

suddenly transformed into a swirled rattler
who pities me briefly in my blindness
so proud to be upright, advancing
the snake stares through me unthreatened

I move forward still innocent, curious
she swirls the tail *vibrato segundo*
allows me a second chance

every fiber capable of tautness rises up
at my feet I see it visceral and clear
the desolation of an incomplete checklist
lying abandoned by the trail
the awful, awe of impermanence in every instant
sways at the deadly grace-gate of nature

we notice our every movement
I build on the spot a cairn
a eulogy for the moment-passed
a paean to perception
the sudden realization
I am so close to crawling on my belly
cells mingling with the canyon dust

the rest of the trip, spectacularly uneventful
over patches of dark green seeps
graying lichen patches on ebony rocks
to the Rufous-capped Warbler so fresh and lusty
a minute Garuda brags from the tops of scrub-oaks

beyond connections at the head of a canyon
I discover notes under stones
faded hieroglyphs from bird seekers
now, reduced to scrabbling on the walls
about the delight of discovery
the disillusionment of no-bird
were they ignorant of how close it was for them?
had the fangs of Awareness grazed them unnoticed?

I write pompously, but sincerely
on a page from my notebook

> *The relief of survival is humbleness, not gratitude*
> *Nothing owes you any more*
> *All debts are forgiven*
> *All entitlements released*

Never count on the pity
Never rely on the tears
    of nature
    of phenomena
Never threatened by the dimness
the coiled serpent of brilliance reigns

and place it, carefully, cautiously, under a rock

yes, I had been bitten
but I walk out with the world
past the cairn, where she wraps herself
    in a low hanging branch
I bow, just low enough to face her eyes once more

the choir of Black-throated Sparrows
unseen from the shallowing hillsides
chants the recessional
I pass out below
ushered by the geologic flow
to a landscape crowned by ocotillo
beyond the receding crimson walls
a quartet of Blue Grosbeaks welcomes me
among darting flower-voracious hummers

I waltz between spines of prickly pear
to the rented all-wheel everything
I steer to avoid the insects in the track
with the faint echo of a survivor's guilt
reach for a Kleenex
and ignore the flashing seat belt sign.

                                      August, 1996
                                      Benson, Arizona

Aravaipa Canyon Ambush
(for BHC)

A talkative cowboy impatiently
fusses over a barbwire gate
his horse shows signs of boredom
further on real estate signs
and roadside thistle warn
of an invasion to come

look out over a few ranch buildings
of shrunken gaping wood
roofs of corrugated rust
corrals built when cedar could still
be abundant in these hills
now wander and lean haphazardly
ready to succumb to a nudge

wizened Cottonwoods tap the stream
yield to giant Sycamores with rash-like bark
set off the crumbling red rock hillsides
that hold the space of the canyon
as it narrows, invites us alert

our attention is captured
by an utter absence of expectation
time ceases, anxiety melts
vital arguments held suspended
seized by a triangulated pact with nature

the surge of our awareness
floods the canyon to the rim
in concealed alliance joins
the conspiracy of this place

For we are in this together.

they appear on cue
male and female Buteos circling
husband and wife whistling
across the space between us
wafting up off the cliff-currents
for an even better view

two tail-bands or one
we could care less
but we know
as one alights on the ridge
crossed to join her son

scrag oak under-leaf shimmer
a few juniper give way to a pale purple horizon
captured by the heat
penetrate the haze
on a barren patch of red
the mother Black Hawk in patient pride
whispers secret instructions
to her huge whimpering offspring
the husband wafts calling overhead

And we are linked forever.

the water stands in isolated pools
not abandoned, knowing
in expectant communion for the
consummation of the rain
the overflow of higher springs

In the unity of awe
we share a moment at 52.

August 24, 1997
Aravaipa Canyon, Arizona

Ghosts of Skeleton Canyon

At the end of a trail fading into sparse grasses
Arizona late summer afternoon, looking for gnatcatchers
I stumble into Geronimo's Surrender Site
unmarked unnoticed atrocious heat
desiccated leaves, ears overwhelmed
by the dying saw of winged insects
a lone crazed cow on my left flank
eyes red-rimmed with flies
staggers in her half-ton bewilderment

Ash-throated Flycatcher family fresh to this world
playing close together amid vicious thorn scrub
the sky is blue, with distant thunder
below the flat land holds uncountable hues
of yellow-brown beauty
a smudge along the horizon betrays
the march of climate control across the land

My plastic Evian bottle sloshes only quarter full
twenty-five dollar per day rental car
down the track a risky distance
sunscreen long since perspired away
sore back and gout, ailments I have ignored
rise up to remind me of limits

A Barrel Cactus catches me through the trouser leg
crowned by a ragged blossom
left from the last April's rain
the pain opens my eyes
ever widening, whirling a kaleidoscope
the cow starts, shudders away from me sideways
we are equally undomesticated, delirious
yet there is a strange sense of belonging
I am moved to strip off my shirt and cry out
for this is a place I have been before.

He stood near me here, in 1886
young Lieutenant Gatewood unarmed
empathetic and torn
dying of a cough
amid tall cottonwoods, an oasis for the untamed
where a year-round spring flourished
he risks more than his life to mediate an event
reported to have "ended the Indian Wars forever"

He sees with the clarity of exhaustion
the charade would bring no precious peace
not slice the cycle of hatred
not hold in delicate balance the land

Across there, his eyes locked with Gatewood
ignore the General seated
Geronimo stands, with a band of 35, women and children
the arch enemy of the proclamation of civilization
now adored, then vilified
brown emaciated his face lined deeply
a Mexican saber scar purple
with a defiance become habit
unapologetic yet reflective

How could we have murdered? How could we not!
the odds are overwhelming, our life is extinguished
  before our eyes
as we rage against the fading, the dying
of the pink-orange reflections on cliffs soaring high
  into inaccessible gloom
touched only by lightning containing immortality
  a glimpse of our divinity

A flock of gnatcatchers moves around me
calling to each other above the limits of my hearing
I try to separate them by tail pattern

> *We rode, then ran, and limped as protectors, as its servants unknowing*
> *but always in front of the coming of*
>   *the disconnected ones and their numberless children*
> *Who is able to state who scalped the first*
>   *the first one, red or white?*
> *Who sowed the seed of hatred in the victim's womb*
> *so now which lineage may claim the bloodstained future?*

Neither is deceived but no one understands
it is a charade oft-repeated
one clothed in blue, medals in the sun
one naked in brown, dark eyes flashing
one seated portly, one standing emaciated
each line uttered with habitual conviction
in a tongue unheard by the other

Worthless desert in Arizona for mosquito-ridden swamp
in Florida or wherever, airbrushed in a color brochure
we will pay all your travel expenses
by private railcar for you and your family
if you would just put that rifle down
and put on this free golf shirt
perhaps you prefer the portable TV?

Towns now, Rodeo and Portal
lone outposts on the edge
of your empty domain
live only in fear of themselves
you are the face on the barroom wall
downcast mouth full of lament

is it for the slaughter in defense of La Liberdad
is it that you left these mountains alive
with no gasp of praise for the primordial cliffs
Gatewood is forgotten in an Illinois grave
his memoirs too doubt-ridden
for the biography of conquest

Fabricated heroes from Tombstone to Deadwood
relieve the pain of ambiguity with frontier theater
false fronts, and staged gunfights
Doc Holiday, a tubercular and addicted stand-in
thrives on misappropriated warrior roots
of Cochise, of Mangas, of…

In 1933, Geronimo long dead of grief, regret
in drunken exposure beside some Oklahoma highway
they find the last Apache
a thirteen-year old girl babbling and naked
captured by ranchers in Sonora

> *No one could tell me of her fate*
> *no account of her future is written*
>
> *Now only Trogons visit the spring-fed bottoms*
> *where we passed twice a year in gratitude for a keen life*

Can I break free?
Can I break free?

A Red-tailed Hawk screams
the echo soaring down the rock face
to mix with a thunder roll

The summer's last runoff rages down the draw
obliterates tracks, purges the desert valley
to exhaust itself among grateful once-a-year-fed plants

where men in tight slacks and polished shoes
armed with cell phones
fan out over the landscape
selling 40-acre parcels with view of La Barranca
and vague water rights from the Colorado River.

there is no word "to own" in our language

The gnatcatchers liberate me and move up the draw
I should be thirsty but I am not
as I move easily still shirtless down the track
a disturbing wet spot shows under the car
I suspect it is water, it may be oil or worse
I open the windows and turn off the air-conditioner
until I reach the highway.

August, 1995
Ramsay Canyon, Arizona

Cousin Johnny's Passage
(for JTB)

I

Stopping near Rawlings on Friday
frustrated by the pace at the truck stop
we lapse into the dharma from memory
but there is friction at the edge of the senses
waitress is naïve and plain yet helpful
truckers and what I take for cowboys banter
as if from a script
I am irritated out of place

We fill the Saab at CITGO
amidst canyons of ten-wheels resting
and pulling away from the last city
follow the wagon tracks northwest
nighthawks dance over the highway
caught in the backwash
of a 90 mph immigration from the East

A brief telephone call of your death from the stepson
an invitation to your funeral
no one else in the family would attend
Wyoming was too distant, they said

We could have flown
somehow I was summoned, an urge
to travel that West which lured you here
away from the bondage of family
to pursue your father's myths
a flight along the Oregon Trail
across Muddy Gap, below Hell's Half Acre
and Split Rock, into the Wind River's
a perilous chase down into the heart of the Shoshone

After Virginia Dale there is nothing
but exploding sky
wind-carved mesas lord over undulate green-brown
the Medicine Bow fade to the southeast
shallow prairie sinks illuminate
like gold-rimmed saucers in a flattening light
slanted rays brush mists of dusk
over orange cliffs where junipers
seed and survive in waterless crevasses
twin tracks wend away from a lone post box into nothingness
the next sign reads: "Lamont – Population Three"

II

As a single shot fades away over there
we can see you now
a wanderer crossing the etched horizon
without heirs among the antelope
was it a former life that drew you to
the Washakie to dream?

From the magnetic field of family
the gentility of the Upper Hudson
you were fed on your father's story
oft repeated, sometimes acted out
in the safety of mahogany and velvet curtains
discuss the untamed
mimic the horror
never too close to the barbarous

Then there were the real stories
of divorce and revenge
of choosing sides
and no middle ground

remember the time
your father came to the door
beheld you frigid in the light of kerosene
or you at eight walking down the snow banked drive
sent for food at the country store
so much for eastern plenty
benign aristocratic winters

Thus began the flight from feminine madness
into the embrace of a masculine myth
imposed on you relentlessly
many late nights
at a father's sumptuous table

You fled, arrived to claim for yourself
the ultimate frontier story
told perfectly around a campfire
a sniff of cognac from canvas chairs
beside the trout-laden Popo Agee
of these many stories
I would have picked the same one

III

People flee Wyoming now
birth rate in free fall
called to another American Destiny
abandoned by cattle and oil
coal is now the clown

There was no reasoning why
you wended up to the North Fork
land traded sight-unseen
and IBM shares
for a Park Avenue apartment

Already second generation
you set out roots immediately
without the pain of reconsideration
never to retreat down that canyon
even when your barn
its carefully tended bloodlines burned

IV

Laid out on the lawn in the teepee shade
the ridge you woke to
precise in the cobalt sky
looming over the assembly
you are at rest among bright blankets
still in the portrait-glare of a father
old-looking beyond years, ill-fitting clothes
wind-baked by your adopted prairie
wild black eyebrows move in the breeze

Around you a bewildered reunion of stepchildren
a half-nephew appears from the east
searching for a common reminiscence
among the neighbors
finding neither, here nor there
in the Arapahoe mourning-song

We were mistaken how rich you were
and in the end you called all the bluffs
the chamber empty, you no longer needed to draw
there was little oil in the pickup
penniless and solitary
you neglected your will
for the crossing had been completely accomplished

Portrait miniatures fade beside the trail
as the John Deere mini-loader buries you
adopted in honor in the Shoshone graveyard
you lie down behind the muffler shop
surrounded by adopted families
sheltered by eagles' wings
you perfect your claim to Native soil
you have bartered your pride
for a life of found belonging

V

How did we treat our dead
lying beside the trail of hope
in agony, in starvation
an empty gaze toward the mirage
of the Yellowstone
held in the throes of a gold-dream
fleeing claustrophobia to drown in space

Blessings on them all
that fell in the ruts of their dream
as survivors paused
to turn and pay homage
pressed onward

VI

We return
pulling against a magnet
the usual post-funeral regrets are spoken
so proud for you
we merge
onto the interstate west of Laramie
wondering about a man's legacy
a collection of small-print postcards
lists of ranch-yard birds
and a ledger hidden somewhere

April, 1995
Lander, Wyoming

Bladder Cancer

Standing by the side of the road
Route 17 actually
    urinating once again
Monarch of all I survey
mind flapping in the wind
    icily
over Poncha Pass and down
swirls south wisely to Blanca
carve fresh blown snow edge
the Valley empties
    detoxifies

The space lacks nothing
not the mourning call of the Sandhills
    yet to arrive
the hoped-for migration of Swainson's
    beating upwind from Argentina
or the wail of the ghosts of Fremont's party

Horned Larks flee
between elk-left tufts of prairie grass
Redtails soar from slanted poles
    into a snow-chipped sky
the borrow pit's mysteries decay
    beneath the night's snow
remnants of rusted barbed wire
    strung to a rotted fence line

All hold in weightless suspense
the infinite stories of the old days
    in the Valley
and I smile at my misfortune
    so grave.

February, 2002
Poncha Pass, Colorado

Set up and Take Down or Thank You is Not Enough

I sit in my office again with the dream of Naropa
strangely at peace with the unfinished list
all of the hopes and all of my schemes
stacks of the unfiled irritating
a beeping email in box replete with longings and doubts
memo: "before you go, could you…"
memo: "well you won't be around for this, but…"
Mary Ann protecting on the phone
20 years of an inexhaustible politeness on my behalf
Carmen transcribing my words at a ludicrous pace
Loyally, we band together
So many words hanging in the air, now rushing out the door
some spontaneous, others ferociously planned

I take the Ganesh off the sill
a portentous gift from Kongtrul Rinpoche, my first day on the job
strangely reassuring in his many-headedness
My eyes drift across the room
contemplating His Holiness' pen
Ginsberg's ashes in oatmeal can
the visage of my teachers
some with whom I have never spoken
– the room is full of family

My hand grazes the $59 desk from Target
with all its dignity of re-glued veneer
a hand me down from Dilley
no longer a symbol of humbleness
but a stubborn penuriousness
– that I can not see passing on to Tom
I scan the Sakyong's generous proclamation of Shambhala
thinking what progress have I made for the benefit of sentient beings

I rub the Ganesh desperately again
then over to the painting from Kobun Roshi
– of father and daughter peacocks
a piercing transmission before he passed on
he thought this office too cluttered
and preferred to have business meetings
    in the tea house
to Bayard's watercolor homage to the Manakin dancing in Costa Rica
as the presidency was just a thought
across to Trungpa Rinpoche's caligraphy "AH"
a gift for Allen Ginsberg who had it over his shrine
and Brother Lief bought it at auction to save it from the barbarians
It should go in the library, but the library is not secure
no time for that now – no time for making things secure

The walls echo with the sounds of meetings
of tears, of laughter and endless hopes and fears
and of questions repeated
    How much can we afford?
    How can we not afford?
of inertia, of confusion, of neurosis
and a profound eccentricity I found hard to cover up at this University
just when I thought everything was in order
it would emerge like a drunken calligraphy painted over
with Sherwin Williams paint selection no. 109 – "Academic White"
just when I am most magnificent
pontificating seductively to the accreditation Visiting Team
in walks Tilopa in a loin cloth smelling of rotting fish
only I see him, trying not to be distracted
don't they notice, can't they smell it?
    How did I get this job?

I am so solemn that this 100 year project
may really be a continuing founder's joke on us all
Reflect, project, what happened?
Nothing happened, nothing but learning in a life
slight wisdom gained, friends made, colleagues trained
care too much, who cares
leaving today, yet one never departs
As one faculty said, "Is it a pinnacle or is it just peanuckle?"
Is life going by or are we moving through life?
A kaleidoscope of imaginary events trying to make some sense
a calculus of present moments out of a non sense
I could always cling to dollars and sense
Yes, I know all life is illusion
but why do Naropa U. and all of you seem so vivid
A visualization, an implant of a suggestion of enlightened education
nothing to grab on to, nothing to leave with
all of the poems, all of the speeches
    a whiff of smoke

My eyes fall on dusty blueprints spilling out behind the files
an edifice here and there, an annexation of solid ground
the mind's zoning tested and re-tested
Paramita Campus, Nalanda Hall now 'Something Else' Hall
Oh Sangha House!
Of gifts and debts
a buddhist-inspired monopoly –
– tear down Day House
– put up Nalanda, offend the Nagas, placate the Nagas
– get a bad report from Eva Wong, you have to redo the plans
I am the President of Naropa, and I have to cater
to a youthful black dragon coiling down from the flatirons
I look at the wonderfully professional new recruits
and they are all nodding
    How did I get this job?

And I thought I was a sharp lawyer who had learned every trick
and I am barely on the job for months and Bob Howard sells me a farm
then I borrow eight million because we can't afford not to
or buy the Dairy Queen so we don't have to put up a parking lot
     How did I get this job?

Who is to blame? Is it Bayard?
She dragged me to that first lecture by the Founder in 1974
I shouldn't have sat so close
or maybe any rational person would have left when he was an hour late
He did say: "It is better not to start"
– it wasn't even in small print on the back

We gave and gave and somehow kept getting back
rarely what was expected, but always a good deal
people said I never had a plan
I learned things never went according to plan
Somehow thank-you seems to fall short

3,000 students passing through with us
shaking each hand, signing each diploma
all of whom touching me – no don't worry
I mean teaching me – reaching me
most with love, some with lawsuits, always on the move
they were they are the precious ones, so thankful so graceful
they remain the "echo of my [our] future"

I gaze at my winged chairs still warm from the last visitor
strangely tamed by ten years of conversation, of teachings
of visitors' wisdom shared
of unconditional generosity of heart and mind and wallet
the passion of faculty for art and science and life
the heat of orders given, of orders ignored
– of my hearing my own voice say it has come to an end, enough is enough
– of firing people, of hiring people – confused as to which is best

– of my risking the Founder's bequest
– of my not risking all as he would have
    The brilliance and the sanity
    The confusion and the inanity

Suddenly I am speechless sitting quietly with HH Jigme Phuntsok
    or having Khenpo Rinpoche for tea
sandwiched between them is some new age spiritual materialist
who wants to charge us $15,000 for a lecture on peacemaking
in the Middle East based upon some Peruvian shaman's ritual
he learned at Esalen
Then, the chair is filled by Kongtrul Rinpoche
who just dropped by unannounced for a chat about merit
– the chat that lasts a lifetime
Or Bayard and I are sitting with Ponlop Rinpoche
while Steven Seagal is pulling centuries' old practice implements
out from under his massive Ralph Lauren Tibetan greatcoat
like some tremendous cosmic joke

    How did I get this job?
    How much are they paying me?
I spot the annual fund pledge
– I have forgotten the terms of my contract –
    Am I paying them?
Having been blessed by more dharma in this room
than any bureaucrat has a right to expect
– in ten lifetimes, much less ten years
    somehow thank you is not enough

I look up at Manjushri's sword waving across my room and
    realize the time is now
    the jig is up
Next to him is the Founder so youthful, walking with his teacher
    Khyentse Rinpoche
vigorous and alive, but ageless, not expectant

Me at 59 sitting in America in the president's chair
contemplating the past and time running out
haunted by the transparency of accomplishment
the frightening limitation of impermanence

I look at my back door and recall Simon's line:
"Just step out the back, jack!"
which reminds me of many trips to the bathroom
I feel the stirring of that other teacher, cancer,
and am chilled and thankful for it
Has it returned or is it the vividness of memory of it – also so real
and for the healing power of the community that is Naropa University
and to the accurate friendship of Bayard
she always asking questions, both relative and absolute
that I would never even ask, much less risk answer
My eyes fall on the baby, Jamgong Kongtrul and grandson James
    – at one in a troubled world

How can I dismantle what does not exist?
There is a fireproof safe on sale at Office Max
sorry you can't take it with you
And to all of you, my teachers here tonight
you have accelerated my path
to keep up with the inevitable shortening of time
For all of this and that and more to come
    Thank you is not enough
    – but thank you anyway.

April 12, 2003
Boulder, Colorado

Field Notes

Page 3
The swan is the Mute Swan, *Cygnus olor,* a European bird introduced into North America. Populations have become feral and self-sustaining. It is "domesticated" on ponds, where it has a mixed reputation for undeniable grace and beauty combined with great strength and protectiveness of young and territory, as well as consuming large amounts of food. The young swan, or cygnet, is a darker grayish-brown in the first summer, becoming mostly white by November or December.

Goldfinch refers to the American Goldfinch, *Carduelis tristus,* a finch widespread across the U.S. and southern Canada. The adult breeding male is a vivid yellow-gold with black wings and black cap. It is fond of thistle, and a common visitor to bird feeders that offer it.

Page 4
Female House Finch is the female, *Carpodacus mexicanus,* also a common feeder bird, which is a dull streaky brown, different from the male which presents with an orange-red head and breast. The House Finch was also introduced from Europe and spread rapidly throughout the U.S. from south to north in the second half of the 20th century to become common throughout. It is to be distinguished in the field from the "wilder" members of the same genus, Purple Finch and Cassin's Finch, which presents an identification challenge for beginning birders, in terms of field marks, voice, habitat and, perhaps, behavior.

Page 6
"Leave their nails behind" is a reference to the belief that when an enlightened master dies his or her physical body dissolves and the "wisdom body" remains composed only of a rainbow light or the light of infinite wisdom and only the twenty nails and head hair are left from the physical body. Tibetans and Bon practitioners relate many stories and examples of such auspicious deaths, including people who even their family did not suspect had achieved such a state of realization.

Page 7
Easton Court Hotel (ca. 1450) was owned by my paternal grandmother until she died in the 1960's. She purchased it in the 1930's. She apparently did set out the family silver in the guest dining room.

The inn became a retreat for a band of British writers, the most "famous" of whom was Evelyn Waugh. Among other works, he is reputed to have written *Brideshead Revisited* (1945) at the Easton Court between December 1944 and June 1945. In one of his biographies, he is quoted in a letter mentioning that it was curious because "…one is never presented with a bill." Rather than viewing it as an act of generosity or perhaps deliberate forgetfulness, he viewed it with suspicion, surmising that the inn didn't need money because of cocaine dealing or some such activity. Waugh's arrogance was a more likely reason for his reaction to this kindness rather than the allegation that my grandmother was a drug dealer. By his own admission in wartime 1944–1945 when he was writing *Brideshead,* Waugh was almost totally broke, a condition which he later said colored, perhaps exaggerated, the contrasting opulence of *Brideshead.*

Also staying at Easton Court was Alec Waugh, Evelyn's older brother, an excellent author although somewhat in the shadow of Evelyn's fame. He wrote *Thirteen Such Years at Easton Court,* one of a number of well-received works. Alec Waugh's first book *The Loom of Youth* (1917) was part autobiographical and was controversial, if not condemned, in 1917 because it exposed the homosexual passions of English public school boys at The Sherbourne School in Dorset, England. Alec Waugh remains to this day the only person to have been expelled from the Old Boy's Society of the Sherbourne School. Another bit of lore is that Alec Waugh is credited with having hosted (therefore "invented") the first cocktail party.

Another frequent guest and writer at the inn was Sir Patrick Fermor (1915–   ) whose life story reads like fiction. He is the author of many travel books and novels, including *A Time of Gifts* which some critics called one of the best travel books in the English language. He wrote *The Traveler's Tree* (1950) while staying at the inn.

Page 10
Scorhill Stone Circle, sometimes referred to as the Stonehenge of Dartmoor, near the Village of Chagford, Devon, is one of a group of seven circles sited precisely around the northeastern edge of Dartmoor. These circles were constructed as one linked complex of Bronze Age (ca. 3,000–1,000 B.C.E.) ceremonial activity. Scorhill originally had some 60 stones placed, but, due to its accessibility, only some 34 remain, of which 23 are thought to be in their original positions. Stories abound about Scorhill, and its astronomical alignments, one being that the wild ponies of Dartmoor will not cross into the area enclosed by the circle.

Page 17
The source in the poem is an article, "Déjà vu Again and Again" by Evan Ratliff, *New York Times,* July 2, 2006. The article describes the research work on a diagnosable condition loosely named "déjà vécu" translated "already lived through." One of the patients described in the article gave up tennis "because she knew the outcome of every rally."

Page 21
In saying "My life expectancy is 85," the poem is on the hopeful side because statistically at sixty, one's life expectancy as a white male is approximately 20.6 years or 80.6 years. At sixty five, it increases to 16.9 or almost 82. A white woman's life expectancy is approximately 3.5 years longer than the white male. See *U.S. Life Tables,* National Vital Statistics Reports, Vol. 54, No. 14 (April 19, 2006).

Page 24
If a hydrogen atom was the size of a football stadium, its nucleus would be the size of a marble. The ratio of atom size to nucleus size in the hydrogen atom is 100,000:1 or 0.001%, rather than the 1% in the text. The ratio changes with heavier elements but not radically. The building block of all matter, the atom is mostly space. With the discoveries of quantum physics, even the subatomic particles we took as "solid" in space or time are now suspect.

Approximately 320 species of hummingbird (Family: *Trochilidae*) have been identified, entirely in North and South America, with almost half these species reported to Ecuador. The number changes somewhat depending on the shifting scientific criteria for what constitutes separate "species." The life history of any hummingbird is the stuff of magic: their habits, metabolism, migration patterns, endurance, and the fantastic forms into which individual species have evolved.

Page 27
Les Deux Magots is a café in the St. Germain des Prés area of Paris, renowned for being a rendezvous for artists and intellectuals in the 1920's and 1930's. Now it is mostly a tourist mecca. Les deux magots refer to the two wooden statues of Chinese mandarin traders found in the main room of the café.

Page 34
Nalanda refers to Nalanda University located in Bihar State in northeastern India. From the 5th to the 12th century C.E., Nalanda flourished as one of the principal centers of learning in India and beyond. At its height, it had 10,000 students and 2000 faculty residing and studying a broad curriculum within the campus. Students and faculty came from all parts of Asia. In 1193 A.D., Nalanda was sacked by Muslim invaders from the north. Some sources, including Islamic historians, recount that it took six months to burn the contents of Nalanda's nine-story library. For many historians, this date marks a defining moment in the decline not only of Buddhism in India but also of the preeminence of Indian scientific thought. The ruins have been protected, although not greatly restored. Naropa, the Indian pandit after whom Naropa University is named, was the equivalent of Dean of the Faculty at Nalanda in the mid-12th century.

Padmasambhava, or Guru Rinpoche, refers to the great spiritual teacher and master who brought Buddhism to Tibet in the 8th century. His realization of the teachings was complete, and, as a result, he manifested in magical ways of which stories abound. The places where he appeared and taught are revered as pilgrimage sites throughout Tibet, Nepal, Sikkim and Bhutan. His importance for most Tibetan Buddhists is second only to the Buddha. (See Tak Sang below). He is also known to have left teachings hidden, that they might be "discovered" again at the appropriate time.

Bon refers to the indigenous animistic religion of Tibet which flourished before the arrival of Buddhism. Padmasambhava converted the practitioners of Bon, the Bonpo, to Buddhism. The historical and spiritual relationship of the Bon to Buddhism is extremely complex, especially in terms of which tradition adopted what from whom.

Page 37
Lha is a Tibetan term literally meaning "divine" or "god," but it also refers to the first wakeful quality of the eyes and head, especially the forehead. In hierarchical terms, lha usually refers to the highest point, such as the peak of a mountain. (See Lhasang below.)

Page 41
Bobwhite refers to Northern Bobwhite, *Colinus virginianus,* a member of the quail family. The Bobwhite is a generally secretive resident of the eastern and central United States ranging as far west as eastern Colorado and New Mexico. It is named for, and most people know it by, its whistle, "bob WHITE," distinctive and evocative in the eastern woods. The male, and the slightly duller female, are both strikingly beautiful with patterns of rich reddish-brown and grays, and strongly masked face. Quail have a very short life span averaging less than one year.

Page 42
"A last egret" refers to the Snowy Egret, *Egretta thula,* a very widespread species known for its white plumes and separated by birders from the similar Great Egret by its "golden slippers" or yellow feet at the bottom of long black legs. The Snowy Egret was widely hunted for its feathers in the southeastern United States at the turn of the 20th century to supply plumes for ladies' hats. This hunting reduced their numbers almost to extinction. Protests against the trade in egret feathers resulted in the start of the organized bird conservation movement. For example, the Massachusetts Audubon Society was founded in 1896 by a group of women concerned about the use of birds to supply the women's fashion industry.

Page 47
American Gothic is the title given to the well known portrait by Grant Wood (1891 – 1942) that dates from 1930 and now hangs in The Art Institute of Chicago. It is famous, but often because it is excessively parodied for comedic and commercial purposes. The portrait derives its name from the style of the Iowa farmhouse ("Carpenter Gothic") behind the models who were actually Wood's sister and his dentist. Originally criticized as being demeaning of "country folk", it has since been widely accepted as a strong, if not moody, representation of Midwestern life, of which the precise meaning or the artist's intention is debated. Despite Wood's abilities expressed in a wide range of media, such as ink, charcoal, metal, wood and found objects, he is forever tied to this one work.

Page 49
The Palsgraf Case *(Palsgraf v. Long Island Railroad Co.)* is required reading for first year law students in the field of tort law. The case articulated a limitation on the doctrine of proximate cause, to those plaintiffs whose injury was *reasonably foreseeable* to the negligent actor. However, the opposing doctrine, that all injuries caused by a negligent act no matter how indirect, remote or unforeseeable are actionable, is still debated and sometimes applied by judges, depending often on the sympathetic nature of the plaintiff and the injuries or conversely the unsympathetic nature of the defendant's actions or situation.

Page 51
Bardo is a Tibetan word central to an understanding of Buddhism. It is often translated as "intermediate state" and is the gap between the past and the future, an interval, a sense of openness that can be between thoughts or even between death and rebirth. The teachings on Bardo point out the fundamental continuity of mind throughout our entire experience in life and death, from birth to rebirth. Its common usage is to refer to the period after death, but it is a far broader term.

Page 52
Yellow-rumps refer to the Yellow-rumped Warbler, *Dendroica coronata,* a Wood Warbler widespread in North America during migration and can be found during winter in the southern states. It is often seen in flocks. It is an early migrant in the spring and can be one of the first warblers seen by birders anxiously awaiting signs of spring migration. It used to be two species, Myrtle Warbler in the east with a white throat and Audubon's Warbler in the west with a yellow throat, both with yellow rumps. Although somewhat different in appearance, song and range, they were declared one specie and "lumped" by the American Ornithological Union (AUO) under the name Yellow-rumped Warbler.

The bluebirds are Eastern Bluebirds, *Sialia sialis,* a bird that used to be well-known to home owners throughout the Midwest and eastern U.S. Its population declined for years until vigorous nest box programs appear to have aided its comeback. The same pair, or the offspring of the pair, may return in the spring to the same nest box or tree cavity. The male and female tend to form a strong bond through a breeding season. The behavior described is "ground-sallying," going from a perch to the ground where they might rest for a few seconds to seize an insect, then returning to the same or different perch. There are two other species of bluebird in North America, Mountain Bluebird and Western Bluebird. The latter is similar to the Eastern; however, its population is declining in the western U.S. Bluebirds are members of the Thrush family and, thus, related to the American Robin.

Red-bellied Woodpecker, *Melanerpes carolinus,* is a common large woodpecker of the southeast woodlands. Over the last 50 years, it has spread north into New England and west where it can be found in eastern Colorado. Its call is distinctive, usually heard before the bird is seen. Downy Woodpecker, *Picoides pubescens,* is the smallest woodpecker in the United States and can be seen most everywhere except the Southwest. It is to be distinguished from the slightly larger Hairy Woodpecker, *Picoides villosus.* The Downy's call is a distinctive rattle: *ki ki ki ki ki.* The Downy's drumming, often used as a form of communication in the spring, is very distinctive.

Page 55
Clay-colored *(Spizella pallida)* and Grasshopper Sparrows *(Ammodramus savannarum)* to the non-birder or, perhaps, beginning birder can be discarded as a "little brown bird." With practice, their differences in looks, song and/or habitat become clearer. Grasshopper Sparrow is secretive and usually alone or in pairs. Clay-colored can be found in sizeable flocks in fall and winter. Both species prefer fields and brushy or grassy areas.

Page 56
LeConte's refers to LeConte's Sparrow, *Ammodramus leconteii,* that can be a challenging identification in migration in Iowa or elsewhere due to the similarity of the sparrows of the genus, *Ammodramus,* all of which (except Saltmarsh Sharp-tailed and Seaside Sparrow) can be found in Iowa. LeConte's winters on the Gulf Coast and breeds in the plains of the Canadian provinces as far east as Quebec. The bird is a good find, especially in the late summer or fall when it shows up in surprising places. This bird was likely on its way to Canada or northern Minnesota to breed. This sparrow was "discovered" by John James Audubon and named for his friend, Dr. John LeConte (1818 – 1891) who was a physicist and President of University of California at Berkeley.

Page 57
Coots and Blue Wings refer to American Coot, *Fulica Americana,* and Blue-winged Teal, *Anas discors.* The Coot is not a duck, being closer to Gallinule and Rails. Its behavior is most duck-like however. The Blue-winged Teal is a handsome, delicate duck, widespread throughout North America, breeding in the U.S. and Canada, generally wintering in the southern states and Mexico.

Page 58
Kalona Village is an Amish settlement in eastern Iowa. Old Order Amish began settling in Iowa in the mid 1850's. The Kalona area is now home to the largest Amish Mennonite community west of the Mississippi River. Most people assert that little has changed in their lifestyle for 150 years.

OM, AH, HUM are seed syllables used in a mantra of blessing or purification in Buddhist practices and are directed at the three aspects, of body, speech and mind. *OM* is associated with body, physical form and purifies the physical, both body and the environment. *AH* is associated with speech and purifies sound, communication and expression. *HUM* is associated with mind and heart and purifies thoughts. The three syllables together often introduce longer mantras in Buddhist prayers or invocations.

Page 59
"No longer able to distinguish colors" is derived from a remark by Chögyam Trungpa Rinpoche that a sign of the Dark Age would be the inability of the sight perception and the mind to distinguish one color from another.

Page 61
The quote is from Longchen Rabjam (1308–1363), known as *Longchenpa,* who is revered as one of the greatest scholars of the Nyingma tradition of Tibetan Buddhism. He spent most of his life in solitude, traveling or on retreat. He also wrote some 250 texts, several of which are seminal texts, studied and practiced to this day.

Page 66
Blackburnian Warbler, *Dendroica fusca,* is a Wood Warbler with a striking orange and black head, face and neck. An insectivore, it is usually found feeding high in the canopy of tall trees, making it difficult to see well, although, if seen, not so difficult to identify because of its unique coloration in breeding season. As with other Warbler species, it is often heard before it is seen. Blackburnian Warblers migrate through the Midwest, including Iowa, from Mexico, breeding in south central to eastern Canada and New England. Birding in spring can be more or less difficult depending on whether the foliage comes out early or late in relation to the timing of the migration.

Mount Meru is a mountain sacred to the Hindus, sometimes referred to as the Olympus of the Hindus, reputed to be 80,000 leagues (450 k.m.) high. In Tibetan Buddhism, Mount Meru represents the center of the universe. It is implied that one could undertake a pilgrimage to Mount Meru, if one developed the capacity to find and see it. That Mount Meru is the central point in the complex Hindu and Tibetan cosmology might not be surprising to the student of Greek myth. Mount Meru is often seen in Tibetan iconography, such as tangkas, stupas and sand mandalas.

Page 70
Sand Creek is the site of the surprise attack upon and subsequent massacre of a village of Arapahoe and Southern Cheyenne tribes by Colonel John Chivington and 700 volunteer troops in November 29, 1864. Approximately 150 Indians were killed, most of them women and children. The causes and consequences of the Sand Creek Massacre, which was only briefly hailed as a great victory, are tragic, and also reflect the culture and politics of the west at the time of the Civil War. Sand Creek sowed the seeds for U.S./Native American relations throughout the balance of the 19th century, Little Bighorn, Wounded Knee and beyond. Sand Creek is located in southeastern Colorado.

Wounded Knee refers to the site in South Dakota of the "massacre" (as General Nelson Miles called it) or "battle" between the Miniconjou and Hunkpapa Sioux and the U.S. Army on December 29, 1890 in which about 300 Sioux, men women and children, and 25 soldiers were killed. Much has been written about Wounded Knee. The 71 day occupation in 1973 of the site by members of the American Indian Movement returned it to the public's consciousness. It is now considered by many as one of the greatest atrocities of the U.S. Army upon Native Americans. The fact that twenty Medals of Honor were awarded to soldiers who fought in the action is still salt in the wounds of Native Americans.

Condor refers in this case to the California Condor, *Gymnogyps californianus,* a new world vulture and the largest raptor in the U.S., which by the 1980's was reduced to a non-viable population of about 25 individuals. The last remaining Condors were trapped and made part of an existing captive breeding program. Within the last ten years, individuals raised in captivity have been returned to the wild in the Grand Canyon area. This re-introduction program has met with some success. Condors face many challenges in the wild, not the least of which is the ingestion of lead shot found in carcasses on which they feed, resulting in lead poisoning.

Page 71
The Avocet is the American Avocet, *Recurvirostra americana,* while the stilt is the Black-necked Stilt, *Himantopus mexicanus.* The Avocet and Stilt are in the same Order as sandpipers and plovers and are two of the most delicate, elegant waders to be found in North America, especially at shallow inland wetlands and prairie pools. The Avocet has a long thin upturned bill, bold white and black wings, and in breeding plumage a light brown almost dark peach-colored neck and head. The Stilt has a formal black back and back of the neck, contrasting with bright white of the under parts and red legs. The nesting displays of the Avocet are a complex and beautiful dance.

Red-tail refers to the Red-tailed Hawk, *Buteo jamaicencis,* a widespread North American raptor that is found anywhere in the U.S. and most of Canada, usually seen soaring overhead. This hawk's plumage variations are a source of much conversation among birders, although the majority of individuals can be recognized by a pink-orange-red tail. However, exceptions abound from the very dark morph (Harlan's Red-tailed hawk) to the very light (Krider's Red-tailed Hawk).

The dance of the Grouse refers to the fantastic dancing displays of various species of that family, *Phasianidae,* such as Greater Sage Grouse, *Centrocercus urophasianus,* and Greater Prairie Chicken, *Tympanuchus cupido,* who engage in dawn dances at a central location or lek that involve complex movements and sounds.

Like the Condor, the Whooping Crane, and the little Kirtland's Warbler, the Ivory-billed Woodpecker, *Campephilus principalis,* is perhaps the poster bird for the threat and reality of species' extinction. Habitat loss resulting from development or, in the case of the Ivory-billed, the clear cutting of large tracts of land in the southeast, inexorably leads to the species' disappearance. This large, striking, and secretive woodpecker is the Holy Grail of birders since the last verified sightings in the 1950's. The discovery of another Ivory-billed in the swamps of Arkansas in 2005 produced the most optimistic moment for the bird conservation movement in the last hundred years. The discovery was followed by controversy because of the lack of scientific proof in the form of convincing photos. Other sightings in Florida have now been reported; so the mystery of the "Lord God Bird" continues.

Page 72
The Paddlefish, *Polyodon spathula,* is said to be the oldest surviving animal species in North America. Fossil records argue that it predates the dinosaurs. It inhabits the Mississippi River Basin requiring a strong deep clean river flow. The Paddlefish has a profile like a shark and a long protuberance or nose shaped like a spatula. Like a shark, it has cartilage and no bones. Unlike the shark, it has no teeth and eats plankton using a filtering system. Paddlefish can grow to seven feet in length and some 200 pounds in weight.

Catfish refers to the large family of fish which range worldwide. They are found and fished in rivers and lakes. While they have a reputation for eating carrion or dead things, this is not their primary diet. However, they are omnivores.

Vulture refers to the Condor (see page 70 above) and the two other North American vultures, Black Vulture and Turkey Vulture. They are nature's avian recyclers, feeding almost exclusively on carrion. The greater availability of road kill has led to the Turkey Vulture's expansion into the northeast. All three have bare featherless heads and necks, so as to allow them to probe deeply into carcasses; a practical evolutionary development but an aspect that some feel ugly, if not disquieting.

Page 74

Golden-winged Warbler, *Vermivora chrysoptera,* is also a Wood Warbler, although in a different genus from the Blackburnian (Page 66 above). Like the Blackburnian, it migrates through Iowa in the spring and fall, and is much sought after by birders in May and June, when it is singing and in breeding plumage. For birders in Iowa or along the migration path, this time may be the one chance to get a glimpse of this jewel of a warbler. The male of the species has a bright yellow crown and a wide bright yellow bar on the wing, offset by black throat and auriculars. As does the Blackburnian, the Golden-winged has a high pitched song that is distinctive, but difficult for aging ears losing that higher range of sound sensitivity.

Peregrine refers to the Peregrine Falcon, *Falco peregrinus,* a falcon found throughout the world. It averages about 16 inches in length with a wingspan of 40 inches, but is one of the most powerful birds in the world. Reaching speeds of 175 m.p.h. in a dive, it violently catches birds on the wing. The adult peregrine with dark "mustache" on a white cheek and yellow lores is a visage to be reckoned with. They nest on cliffs, or increasingly, on the tops or window sills of tall buildings where they feast on abundant urban pigeons. Almost eradicated by D.D.T. in the 1950's and '60's, along with the Brown Pelican and the Osprey, they are a remarkable comeback story. The Peregrine mates for life and usually returns to the same nesting location.

Page 76

Ground Dove refers to the Common Ground Dove, *Columbina passerine,* a small ground foraging species found in Florida and southern Texas, as well as the Bahamas, where the author first met his wife "over a Ground Dove" auspiciously walking up the beach.

Rose-breasted Grosbeak, *Pheucticus ludovicianus,* has been called "the robin of the woods," because of its robin-like song and its preference for the deciduous forest. As the name implies, the male of the species has a black head and a bright rosy-red breast with blackish wings with white patches. It breeds in Iowa, but not as far west as Colorado where its niche is occupied by the Black-headed Grosbeak. Where Rose-breasted and Black-headed overlap in range, telling the females or the juveniles apart may present a challenge, further complicated by the fact that the two species often hybridize.

Page 77
"Cathedral has no pews" is a reference to a circumstance in Latin America where indigenous peoples adapt the Catholic church as well as the liturgy, often removing all the pews from the church. The particular example in the poem is San Juan Chamula, a church in the small village of Chamula in Chiapas State, Mexico. The church in Chamula, founded in the 16th century, has had a most interesting evolution producing a vital blend of indigenous customs and practices combined with Catholic ritual, the saints and the veneration of the Madonna.

Bell's Vireo, *Vireo bellii,* is a member of the Vireo Family, a group of foliage-gleaning passerines, similar in size and shape to, but generally less colorful than, warblers. Fifteen species of vireo may be seen in the U.S. Most of the family inhabits Mexico or the southwestern U.S. Bell's Vireo breeds in Iowa, but is local and not easily seen. The location in the poem was unusual for Bell's Vireo; probably the bird had just arrived exhausted from migration. It winters in Mexico and Baja. A long tail is one of the distinguishing field marks of this species, along with a distinct song.

Page 78
Dharma is a Sanskrit word generally associated with religions originating in India although some assert it has European language roots. In Buddhism, it has two basic meanings: "teachings of the Buddha" and "truth" or "the way things are." Along with words such as *mantra* and *karma,* it has become part of the English lexicon.

Page 81
Zendo is a Japanese word that loosely translates as meditation hall.

CJB is Charlotte Joko Beck a long time American Zen practitioner and teacher and author of two excellent books, *Everyday Zen* and *Nothing Special.*

Solitaire is Townsend's Solitaire, *Myadestes townsendii,* a thrush-sized bird of the coniferous forest usually at higher altitudes, as in this case at 8,500 feet. In the Rockies, it often sits at the top of a Ponderosa Pine and gives a rich warbling song or its call, a very clear one note whistle given at random but well-spaced intervals. Morning Robin refers to the American Robin, related to the Solitaire but different in behavior and appearance and far more widespread and common.

Page 85
Mala is a Sanskrit word meaning literally "garland" or "necklace" and is a string of beads, usually 108 in number, used primarily in the recitation of a *mantra,* another Sanskrit word meaning "mind protection." Both words have a complex significance in eastern religions, but, practically speaking, the mala is used to keep track of the number of repetitions of a mantra (e.g. *Om, Ah, Hum*). The intention may be different, but the use is somewhat parallel to the Catholic rosary.

The hawk-cuckoo was probably Common Hawk Cuckoo, *Hierococcyx varius.* Hawk cuckoos often sit near the tops of tall trees hidden in dense foliage and call incessantly. This habit has earned this bird the name "brain fever bird," for the effect the call has on the listener. They are parasites, laying their eggs in other birds' nests. Often, native peoples ascribe portentous powers to these birds.

Lhasang burner is a container where juniper smoke is produced as part of a *Lhasang* ceremony, usually a ceremony to attract energy and blessings to the environment and the participants. (See *Lha* above.) A lhasang is often conducted at the top of a mountain or other high place or as a purification ceremony, perhaps at the start of a new venture or building project.

Page 86
Lake Ketcheopalri (or Ketchopari), often called the "wishing lake," is located in western Sikkim (the former kingdom now an Indian state) near Pemayangtse and is a well-known pilgrimage site for both Hindu and Buddhist. As is often true with Asian pilgrimage, the drive in to the trailhead for the lake is a "pilgrimage" by itself. It is said the birds do not allow a single leaf to rest on the lake despite the sizeable uncut forest that surrounds it. There is a Lepcha (the aboriginal inhabitants of Sikkim) village near the lake.

The golden ducks are a pair of Ruddy Shelducks, *Tadorna ferruginea,* which, as the Latin name implies, are perhaps more ferruginous than golden. Their heads, however, are golden-colored and the whole effect, in the right light, gleams golden.

Page 88
Puja is a Sanskrit word meaning "reverence" or "worship" and in this case signifies a Buddhist ceremony or liturgy performed on a particular day and/or for a particular purpose.

The Eagle of St. John is the symbol of St. John the Evangelist, said to be the author of the Fourth Gospel, "The Gospel According to John." The eagle is further said to represent the all-seeing nature of God.

Page 89
Egyptian Vulture, *Neophron percnopterus,* is a magnificent black and white winged bird with a naked face set in a feathered yellow head. It is a widespread Eurasian bird seen in the Pyrenees as well as the Himalayas, Africa and the Middle East. Aside from carrion, they prefer eggs, especially ostrich eggs in Africa. They are one of the few animals that use tools and are seen attempting to drop rocks on eggs to break them open. This process, hopefully, is evolving as their aim is reported to be rather wild. Their eyesight is remarkable, able to pick out small objects on the ground from great heights.

Page 90
Lungta means literally "wind horse" in Tibetan and is a powerful symbol of the innate energy of the phenomenal world and cultivated capacity of all human beings to ride this energy.

Page 91
Vajrayogini is a female "deity" or *dakini* associated with the Tantric practices of the Kagyu lineage of Tibetan Buddhism. She manifests as the highest realization of wisdom and compassion. She also has the capacity for "appearing" when she is most needed, but often in provocative even repulsive forms.

Kora is the clockwise circumambulation of a sacred site, usually a stupa. Kora is widely practiced in Asia as a daily or a pilgrimage ritual. It can be relatively short and done repetitively or as a long journey, such as the kora around Mount Kailash in Tibet. The reference to 108 times is the number of beads on a mala and is generally the multiple used in Buddhist repetitive practices, such as mantra practice. There are many possible reasons for the number 108. Generally, one hundred times is complete, and the eight "extra" are to cover "errors and omissions" in the practice of the one hundred.

Page 93
Dilgo Khentse is the revered Tibetan teacher and meditation master, H.H. Dilgo Khentse, Rinpoche (1910–1991). He was renowned for the joinder of the scholarly with experiential, meditative accomplishment, and his ability to transmit this wisdom to any audience. He taught widely, including in the West, until his death. He was a strong proponent of the Rimé (non sectarian) movement in Tibet. Many of the current generation of Tibetan teachers, including the current Dalai Lama, studied with Khentse, Rinpoche. He resided in Bhutan as well as Nepal and was the teacher to the Queen Mother of Bhutan. His reincarnation has been found and lives in Nepal.

Page 94-95
The Rinpoche referred to in the two poems is Ringu Tulku, Rinpoche, himself a Khampa, having been born there and escaping at the age of four with his family. Khampas originate from Kham a large province of eastern Tibet, from where many great teachers originated, including Chögyam Trungpa, Rinpoche. Khampas are great horsemen, and view themselves as wilder and stronger than other Tibetans. They are considered taller and have different features than other Tibetans and Chinese. Alexandra David-Neel called them "Gentlemen Brigands" and Marco Polo recorded "they were thieves and caravan raiders, practicing all sorts of magic." They were the Tibetans who put up the armed resistance to the Chinese in the 1950's, at times with the erratic support of the C.I.A., and with devastating results for their numbers as well as their many monasteries.

Page 96
Amrita is a Sanskrit word meaning "deathless" or "without death" and usually refers to a purified or sanctified nectar that is involved in Buddhist and Hindu rituals.

The Cave at Tak Sang, meaning Tiger's Nest, is one of the most famous pilgrimage sites in Bhutan as well as the most photographed, perched high on the side of a sheer 4,000 foot cliff. Padmasambhava or Guru Rinpoche is said to have gone to Tak Sang, flying to it on the back of a pregnant tigress.

Page 97
Garuda in Tibetan is a mythical bird of great power and strength, representing the capacity of the mind when liberated from the limitation of thought. Often, the Garuda is represented with a snake in its talons or beak, as it is the enemy of diseases caused by the Naga, the serpent. Garudas are seen in the sculpture and iconography throughout Asia, including the stone carvings of Angkor Wat.

The Black Eagle, *Ictinaetus malayensis,* is, as the name indicates, a very large all black eagle with broad wings with primary feathers spread wide like fingers. Its flight display often involves steep dives in a U-shaped flight pattern.

Page 98
La Transhumance refers to the seasonal vertical migration of families and their livestock (cows and sheep) in the Alps and in this case the Pyrenees, upwards to mountain pastures in the Spring and back to the valley for the winter. The migration often takes weeks and is often associated with a festival or fair in the spring. Until recently, the journey was always made on foot, but the use of large trucks has changed the nature of the important social ritual.

Page 99
Lammergeier (sometimes Lammergeyer), *Gypaetus barbatus,* or Bearded Vulture, inhabits, and breeds, in high mountains of Tibet, Asia, southern Europe (where it is uncommon) and Africa. It is huge, with a wingspan of up to nine feet. Unlike most vultures, it has a feathered head and uniquely eats bone marrow. Thus, it is the last to exploit a carcass. Another name for this bird is Ossifrage or Bone Crusher, due to its habit of dropping bones from great heights on to the rocks to shatter them and obtain the marrow.

Page 101
The quote in French is taken from a gravestone in the small cemetery near the church, Notre Dame du Bon Port, in Gavarnie, France. The author translates it as follows: "From the pure summits of the most difficult mountains of which he loved the grand horizons and the dangers, he has departed for the eternal summits never having known the shadows of the valley."

Page 103
RTR is Ringu Tulku, Rinpoche. See notes for pages 94-95 above.

Page 104
CTR is the Vidyadhara Chögyam Trungpa, Rinpoche (1939–1987) who, among many other accomplishments, was the founder of Naropa University (then Institute) in 1974.

Page 107
White Pelican, *Pelicanus erythrorhynchos,* is one of two pelican species found in North America, the other being the Brown Pelican. The White Pelican breeds on inland lakes and reservoirs in Canada and locally in the U.S. and winters in

Mexico. The Brown Pelican is found along the coasts. Their feeding behavior is very different. The Brown Pelican dives for its catch while the White Pelican feeds in flocks from the surface, driving the fish into shallow water. As should be obvious, a White Pelican would not ordinarily stay behind to spend January in Boulder, Colorado.

Ring-bills are Ring-bill Gulls, *Larus delawarensis,* a widespread and common gull that can be found on inland lakes as well as both oceans.

Scarlet Ibis, *Eudocimus ruber,* refers to an ibis species resident in South America and Trinidad and Tobago that is entirely scarlet with black wingtips. They create a beautiful spectacle as they fly in large flocks at sunset to roost in trees in the tropics.

Page 113
Red Jungle Fowl, *Gallus gallus,* is the wild equivalent of a domestic rooster.

Page 118
Lake Elementeita is located in the part of the Rift Valley that runs through Kenya and is one of the Soda Lakes, so called because of the high mineral content. The waters are caustic, although full of wading birds. The Rift Valley has been a center of anthropological discovery, including the work of Richard and Mary Leakey.

Page 119
Lord Cole's phallus-tomb is the tomb of, or memorial to, Lord Galbraith Cole a turn of the 20th century British settler in the Rift Valley, along with Lord Delamere and Karen Blixen (Isak Dinesen) of Out of Africa fame. Lord Cole at one time owned all of Lake Elementeita and in 1913 built a huge house overlooking the Lake. It is now a hotel, and the lake a reserve. His tomb, a large pointed obelisk, was built on his property on a rock outcrop which continues to "lord" over the region. This reference is also to the British society in Kenya in the 1930's that became notorious for its indolence and amoral behavior. In a sense, English expatriates took advantage of Kenya, and specifically the Rift Valley (an area of which came to be known as "Happy Valley") to "carry on" out of the reach of Victorian society. This period of time is described in a book called *White Mischief* by James Fox. The author admits, other than being in his house, walking his lands and visiting his tomb, he knows nothing about Lord Cole's personal behavior but is merely using "guilt by association" for poetic purposes.

Crowned Plover is a common bird of the African savannah. Spurfowl refers to Red-necked Spurfowl, *Francolinus afer,* a francolin common to Kenya. Two species of pelican are present at Lake Elementeita and can be seen soaring at high altitude over the lake: Great White Pelican and Pink-backed Pelican.

Page 120
John Hanning Speke (1827–64) joined Sir Richard Burton (1821–1890) in his expeditions to Somaliland (1854) and to east central Africa. Together, they discovered Lake Tanganyika; after which, Speke continued alone and discovered Lake Victoria, which he believed to be a source of the Nile. In 1862 he returned

to the lake and proved that the Victoria Nile issued from the north end over Ripon Falls. The relationship between Burton and Speke has been written about extensively, culminating in Alan Morehead's *White Nile* in 1960 and in film, with *Mountains of the Moon*. The lesser known travels of Speke were in the Himalayas where he ventured into Tibet. Speke died of self-inflicted wounds. Burton wrote well and memorialized, if not romanticized, his explorations. He was socially a very controversial figure in Victorian England, due primarily to his interest in sexual habits and pornography. Stanley is Sir Henry Morton Stanley (1841–1904) who is most famous for "Dr. Livingstone, I presume." He led numerous expeditions and was well known for his bravery but also his cruel treatment of the Africans. All three men represent the many facets, brave and cruel, of colonial Britain in the Africa of the 19th century.

Page 126
The nuthatch is *Sitta europea,* the European nuthatch that breeds in central and southern England.

Page 127
The dipper is the White-throated Dipper, *Clincus clincus,* or just Dipper in Europe, a member of the family of small birds that have evolved to walk or dive and feed under the water, usually in swiftly flowing streams. Thus, they are always found near the edge or in moving water.

Page 128
Toul Sleng is seen translated in two ways: most commonly as "Hill of the Poisoned Tree" (or Poisonous Hill) as there are two indigenous trees described by the word, *sleng,* when used as a noun. However, when sleng is used as an adjective, it is translated as "bearing guilt" or "bearing poison" and in that way, the phrase may be translated as "a place to keep those who bear or supply guilt." Some tourist guidebooks refer to it as "Auschwitz on the Mekong" although the author (never having visited Auschwitz) might say that melding the two sites together tends to blur their vivid and horrible distinctions.

Toul Sleng was originally a high school. During the Khmer Rouge period (1975–78), Toul Sleng (also known officially as "S-21") was converted into one of approximately 160 or more such installations, each with an adjacent "killing field," throughout the country. It is estimated that, in less than three years, 14,000 to 20,000 prisoners were tortured at Toul Sleng until they "confessed" and then all were taken out to the nearby killing field and executed (if they did not die during torture at the prison). Of those, only seven people are known to have survived, and, of those seven, only three survive today. Toul Sleng was preserved as it was found as a museum, at the behest of the Vietnamese occupation government and with German funds. There is now an ongoing debate as to whether to tear it down.

Page 129
Year Zero is the name given by the Khmer Rouge to the year 1975 in which they took over Cambodia.

"To tell the truth you need not remember anything," is a quote attributed to Mark Twain.

Page 130
Don't tell me it has always been this way! is derived from a response in 2004 to a question asked of H.E. Tai Situ, Rinpoche by a student who bemoaned the perceived trend that the world seemed more hostile and unkind and wracked by genocide, war, and famine. His immediate and unhesitating response was, "It has always been this way."

"Nous pouvons construire à la liberté un temple ou un tombeau des mêmes pierres" is taken from *Les Main Sales* by Jean-Paul Sartre. The author translates it as: We can build to freedom (liberty) a temple or a tomb of (with) the same stones.

The Toul Sleng Prison authorities kept extensive records of their activities with each prisoner photographed and numbered at the beginning, each signed confession filed, and a record kept, often accompanied by photographs, of the various stages of a prisoner's stay from admission until execution. The reasons for this obsession with making a record of their crimes, I leave to the reader's further investigation. However, from a prosecutor's point of view, the trial of the prison hierarchy would not lack for direct evidence. Certain of the survivors were artists who, ironically, were kept alive because of their skills at painting portraits of the leaders, including Pol Pot. Later, one in particular, Vann Nath, returned and painted scenes of "life" at the prison from memory. Vann Nath survives and lives in Phnom Penh.

Page 132
Duch is the name given to the Commandant of the prison through the entire period, who only recently was put in jail but has yet to be brought to trial. Comrade Duch's real name was Kang Kek Ieu. He was formerly a mathematics teacher. He was arrested as a communist in 1964 and, after being released, disappeared into the forests of Cambodia, until he resurfaced as the Toul Sleng Director. Among his compendium of egregious crimes, when the Vietnamese were advancing on Phnom Penh in 1978 Duch is said to have stayed behind at considerable personal risk to make sure that all the remaining prisoners at S-21 were tortured and killed. Thus, none were liberated by the Vietnamese.

Page 137
Gwynedd refers to the ancient (beginning in the 5th century CE) and medieval kingdom in northwestern Wales which was, depending on its ruler, a dominant and independent kingdom in northwest Wales. Gwynedd resisted English annexation until the 13th century and, thereafter, regularly rebelled against English rule.

Page 138
Fulmar is the Northern Fulmar, *Fulmaris glacialis,* a relative of the albatross and common seabird of the northern Atlantic. Somewhat surprisingly, Fulmar populations have greatly increased over the last century. They nest on island cliffs in large colonies. They are one of the longest lived birds, sometimes breeding at 50 years of age or more.

Murre is the Common Murre (often called a Guillemot in England), *Uria aalge,* a sea bird that also nests on cliffs in the Atlantic and winters at sea. An extremely handsome black and white bird, it reminds one of a small pelican. It is a powerful swimmer and catches fish underwater. Its eggs are very pointed so they roll in a circle believed to be evolved to keep the eggs from rolling off a cliff ledge.

Page 139
Razorbills refers to the Razorbill Auk or Razorbill, *Alca torda,* and like the Murre dives after fish. It is a very handsome yet slightly odd shaped bird with precise black and white plumage and a heavy auk-like bill with sharp white markings.

Page 140
The shearwaters described are Manx Shearwaters, *Puffinus puffinus,* who breed on Skomer Island and nest in burrows by the tens of thousands. They are sea birds and practically unable to move on the land, so they come back from the sea in the evening after dark and leave before dawn. It is somewhat of a mystery how each returning shearwater is able to locate its own burrow. Fledglings that do not make it to the edge of the cliff before light are usually easy prey for their main predator, the Great Black-backed Gull, who begins to hunt after dawn. Manx Shearwaters winter at sea in the South Atlantic.

Page 142
Pentre Ifan, literally Ifan's or Ivan's Village, located in Pembrokeshire, Wales, is said to date from 3,500 to 4,000 B.C.E. It was probably a burial chamber for a Bronze Age tribe. The capstone weighs over 16 tons and is over 17 feet in length, delicately placed on top of three pointed stones raising it 8 feet high. Many myths involve the site, including the story that it may have been used for initiation rites for neophyte Druids. Little People have been seen in the vicinity.

Page 147
Harlequin Duck, *Histrionicus histrionicus,* an uncommon sea duck, is one of the most colorful ducks in the world and inhabits some of the roughest remotest northern sea and inland waters in North America. In the winter it thrives in the rough water of the Atlantic. It breeds on streams and lakes in Iceland, Greenland, Northern Canada and Alaska.

Gannet is the Northern Gannet, *Morus bassanus,* another pelagic species that nest in island cliff colonies and winter at sea. They are large birds with a six foot wingspan. They are strong fliers and spectacular divers from high up, penetrating the sea without a splash, and pursuing their prey underwater. In adult breeding plumage, they are strikingly handsome, all white with black wingtips and a creamy yellow head and blue bill.

Page 151
Purple sandpiper, *Calidris maritime,* is a medium sized sandpiper, an inhabitant of rocky sea coasts. It breeds in and around Baffin Island in extreme northeastern Canada and winters along the New England coastline as far south as the Carolinas.

Page 153
Long-tailed Duck f/k/a Old Squaw is a sea duck, the male of the species with long pointed central tail feathers. Its range, both winter and summer, is in the north, breeding in far northern Canada and Alaska and wintering along the coasts from the Aleutians to Northern California on the Pacific side and from Labrador to the Middle Atlantic coast on the Atlantic side. The duck used to be called Oldsquaw, but its name was changed to Long-tailed, allegedly for the reason of worldwide consistency. Whether political correctness played a role, I leave to the reader's further research. Over recent years with the increasing consciousness and sensitivity to the global nature of birds, local and regional names have tended to disappear. Birders attached to a name are often disappointed, if not enraged, by these changes. The particular intimacy of a local name connects to the social or cultural or historical significance of the bird in question. In the case of long-tailed duck, it was apparently first called Old Squaw by the Eskimos, allegedly because of its wide variety of vocalizations that reminded one of women chatting. Because of its inferred personality, the duck has a long list of local appellations ranging from "callithumpian duck" to "uncle huldy."

Page 159
Neruda refers to the Chilean poet, Pablo Neruda (1904–1973) who, among many other honors, received the Nobel Prize for Literature in 1971.

Page 163
The bird in this poem is the Golden Eagle, Aquila chrysaetos, a thirty inch tall eagle with a seventy inch wingspan and called "golden" because of his golden nape.

Page 164
"Road to Damascus" refers to the encounter and conversion of Saul on the road from Jerusalem to Damascus, where by the biblical account he was struck down by "a light from heaven, above the brightness of the sun, shining round about me..." and received a direct command from Jesus. Acts, 26:13. When he rose to his feet, Saul was blind and remained so for a number of days. He, renamed Paul, went from being the greatest persecutor of all things Christian to one of the greatest Apostles and missionaries to the nonbeliever.

Page 164
The San Luis Valley in south central Colorado at 7,500–8,000 feet is one of the highest arable valleys in the world and sits atop a great underground aquifer capped by a layer of clay. At a certain depth the water is extremely hot, accounting for the number of hot springs in the valley.

Page 166
Two southwestern desert birds, Black-throated, *Amphispiza bilineata,* and Black-chinned Sparrow, *Spizella atrogularis,* can both be seen and heard at French Joe Canyon with the Black-throated being more common and richer voiced. Black-chinned, the duller of the two, is much sought after by birders because its range in the U.S. is very confined. Dusky-capped Flycatcher, *Myarchus tuberculifer,* is likewise a bird that in the U.S. is rarely seen outside of the Arizona border area. These birds and many others make French Joe Canyon a destination for birders. However, it has been the presence of the Rufous-capped Warbler, *Basileuterus rufifrons,* at the head of the canyon in recent years that has drawn heightened attention to this ornithological pilgrimage.

Rufous-capped Warbler is a Mexican and central American species of warbler that is rarely seen in the U.S. In recent years, it has been found almost annually in locations in Arizona. On occasion, a breeding pair has been spotted. It is a lovely olive backed, yellow breasted warbler with rufous patch around the eye separated by a bright white eye stripe. It flaunts a raised and active tail which gives it a boisterous appearance.

Page 168
Blue grosbeak, *Guiraca caerulea,* related closely to the Rose-breasted Grosbeak above, has a lovely rich warbling song and, as the name indicates, the male of the species is a dark blue with reddish brown wing bars. The Beryline Hummingbird, *Amazilla beryline,* is also a Mexican species that has been known to wander post breeding into the U.S., Arizona and west Texas.

Page 169
Aravaipa Canyon is located in Southeastern Arizona, northeast of Tucson and is a birder's destination, having hosted several uncommon raptors over the years in addition to being a beautiful red rock Arizona canyon with year-round stream. The hawk family described is the Common Black Hawk, *Buteogallus anthacinus,* a very uncommon bird in the U.S. One can see other Central American raptors, Zone-tailed hawk and Gray Hawk, in the canyon as well. "Two tail bands or one" is a reference to one of the field marks used to distinguish this hawk from its cousin the Great Black Hawk that is not seen in the U.S. and from the Zone-tailed Hawk mentioned above.

Page 171
The Skeleton Canyon surrender site is in the Pelloncillo Mountains of Arizona. Originally called Cañón Bonita by the Mexicans, it came to be named for a massacre of a Mexican mule train by a gang of bandits (allegedly the infamous Clanton family and associates) who left their victims to rot in the sun. There continue to be rumors of gold from the robbery buried in the vicinity. However, it is better known as the site of Geronimo's final surrender to General Miles in 1886. The site is marked by a sign on the highway, but the actual surrender took place far east of the sign, near the New Mexico border. It is said that a day spent hiking in Skeleton Canyon will show by the experience why it was so difficult

for the army to defeat the Chiricahua Apache. The Apache used it as an escape route (to Mexico) in which they could turn and use the topography to advantage to ambush any pursuers with devastating results. The year before the surrender, in 1885, a troop of cavalry had been caught in an ambush there. Although General Miles took the credit, it was Lt. Charles C. Gatewood who tracked down Geronimo in Mexico and persuaded him to surrender to General Miles at the meeting at Skeleton Canyon. General Miles, thereafter, shows up as the commanding general at Wounded Knee. (See notes for page 70 above)

There are three gnatcatcher species in Arizona, in order of rarity in the U.S.: the Blue-gray, the Black-tailed and the Black-capped. The latter species is much sought after by birders trying to "list" it within the U.S. Gnatcatchers are generally differentiated by different tail patterns on their long tails as they move rapidly, often flicking their tail, through desert scrub, a challenge only birders may appreciate.

Ash-throated Flycatcher is another Arizona species of the *Myarchus* family, like the Dusky-capped described above.

Page 182
Sandhills refers to the Sandhill Crane, *Grus canadiensis,* an almost four foot tall crane that migrates through the San Luis Valley in large flocks. Some flocks use the Valley as a resting point on the way to Canadian breeding grounds. Their bugling call in flight and on the ground is haunting. These cranes are well known for huge congregations along the Platte River in Nebraska, a major attraction for birders and non-birders alike.

Swainson's Hawk, like the Red-tailed, is a Buteo with a buoyant flight. It winters in South America and migrates, usually in flocks, into the western U.S. to breed. In recent years its populations have suffered greatly from the use of lethal pesticides in South America, which infect the grasshoppers it feeds on by the thousands. Pressure on agribusiness has turned the situation around rather quickly.

Fremont's party refers to the ill fated expedition led by the famous explorer and soldier/politician, John C. Fremont in the winter of 1848. Fremont, already an accomplished but arrogant explorer, was trying to prove that one could cross the San Juan Mountains, forming the western barrier of the San Luis Valley, in winter. In the first expedition of 1848, Fremont's party became stranded by blizzards and impassable snows and terrain in the La Garita mountains. One third of his men died. Fremont was to lead a total of five expeditions, none of which would prove his point, but none of which was as disastrous as 1848.

Horned Larks, *Eremophila alpestris,* are widespread larks often encountered on or close to the ground in sizeable flocks in the Colorado prairie in winter. They are the only member of the lark family native to the U.S. They do indeed have feather tufts on the head that appear as tiny horns.

About the Author
John Whitehouse Cobb

Mr. Cobb holds degrees from Harvard College and Columbia Law School. He practiced law for twenty-three years before a curious set of circumstances led to his appointment as President of The Naropa Institute that became Naropa University during the decade of his tenure. His previous book of poems was *Searching for the Moment: Poems on Occasion at Naropa University*. He is the proud holder of an Honorary MFA from the Jack Kerouac School of Disembodied Poetics at Naropa University. He lives with his wife Bayard in the mountains outside of Boulder, Colorado.